IAN RAMSEY

CONTEMPORARY
RELIGIOUS THINKERS SERIES
Edited by H. D. Lewis

IAN RAMSEY

To Speak Responsibly of God

Jerry H. Gill
Professor of Philosophy,
Eckerd College, Florida

London   George Allen & Unwin Ltd
Ruskin House   Museum Street

ISBN 0 04 230014 2

Printed in Great Britain
in 10 point Times type
by Clarke, Doble & Brendon Ltd
Plymouth

General Editor's Note on the Series

This series sets out to provide a critical assessment of the work of some of the most notable and influential religious thinkers of today. It is intended mainly for students and laymen seriously interested in the study of religion. The authors will vary in the degree of their own sympathy with the thinkers they discuss, and scope will be given to them to make a distinctive contribution of their own to the topics they examine.

The writers discussed in the series will include, in addition to informative thinkers in Europe and the Western world, some notable Eastern writers of today. There will thus be made available to our readers some instructive critical comment on writers with whom they may not otherwise have much acquaintance.

For JEREMY

Preface

The importance and value of the late Bishop Ian Ramsey's philosophical and theological thought speaks for itself. However, since his writings are many and diverse, and since he never produced anything like an integrated, systematic work, there is distinct value in a volume which seeks to bring together the major themes of his thought. I am honoured by the opportunity to attempt this in the present manuscript. I should add that Bishop Ramsey read and discussed most of this manuscript with me several years ago, and was satisfied that it presents his views fairly.

I am deeply indebted to Bishop Ramsey's efforts to bring philosophy and theology together in such a way as to cast light on both endeavours. Working with his thought is a first-rate education in the difficulties and benefits of both disciplines. Moreover, the particular thrust of his approach seems to me to be especially fruitful. Thus, I am grateful for the opportunity to contribute to its further understanding.

Since the completion of this present manuscript, Sheldon Press has published (1974) a collection of Bishop Ramsey's more important essays, gathered from a number of philosophical and theological journals, under the title *Christian Empiricism*. This volume contains most of Ramsey's articles referred to in the present manuscript.

I hope that my efforts will express, however inadequately, something of my indebtedness to Ian Ramsey, who above everything else was a dear friend.

15 May 1974   J.H.G.

Contents

Contents

Biographical Note

Ian Thomas Ramsey was born in Bolton, England in 1915. After completing his studies at Cambridge—Firsts in Mathematics (1936), Moral Sciences (1938) and Theology (1939)—he served in minor posts at both Oxford and Cambridge. In 1951 he became Nolloth Professor of the Christian Religion at Oxford and a Fellow of Oriel College. While at Oxford Professor Ramsey was also very active in church matters, serving as Canon Theologian of Leicester Cathedral and taking part in many ecclesiastical, service-orientated projects.

During his years at Oxford he laboured constantly on the frontier between contemporary philosophy and Christian thought, trying to shed light in both directions at once. In addition to lecturing and tutoring many students, he published a number of articles and books dealing with the logical character of the religious use of language, especially in the light of the insights and shortcomings of contemporary empiricism.

Appointed Bishop of Durham in 1966, Ramsey brought the same vigour and broadness of mind to his ecclesiastical responsibilities as he had to his academic ones. He was very deeply involved at the local level of his church work, becoming well known among the people as one who always had time for them. At the same time he served on innumerable committees at high levels in the Church of England and took an active part in the House of Lords. He was thought by many to be the likely successor to the Archbishop of Canterbury. He died on 6 October 1972.

(For a more complete biography see David Edwards, *Ian Ramsey*, London, Oxford University Press, 1973.)

Part One

INTRODUCTION
CHALLENGE AND RESPONSE

Chapter 1

THE CHALLENGE OF LOGICAL EMPIRICISM

Traditionally the relation between philosophy and religion has been viewed either as one of harmony, as in the early Middle Ages, or as one of hostility, as in the Age of Reason. In the eighteenth and nineteenth centuries this hostility often focused on the question of whether the claims of religion were true, and the task of the Christian philosopher was to show that the claims expressed in religious language were indeed true.

Within the last thirty years the situation has been transformed by the rise of the philosophical movement often known as logical empiricism. In the light of the vast and profound influence of this movement, the philosophical world presented a completely different challenge to those who make religious statements. Religious language was no longer classified as false; it was now classified as meaningless. The relation between philosophy and religion was no longer one of positive hostility; the former simply ignored the latter as 'non-sense'. It is the purpose of this chapter to trace briefly how this situation developed. Three phases of the development will be distinguished: the 'logical positivist' phase, focusing on verification as the criterion of meaning; the 'logical empiricist' phase, focusing on falsification as the criterion of meaning; and the 'linguistic analysis' phase, focusing on concrete use as the criterion of meaning.[1]

1 THE LOGICAL POSITIVIST PHASE

The twentieth century has been characterised as 'The Age of Analysis',[2] and with good reason. The one unifying factor of contemporary philosophy is a mood of discontent with the traditional approaches to philosophy in general, and with the absolute idealism of the nineteenth century in particular. This mood was especially intense in the early years of this century, when a veritable revolution took place in philosophy. In the past, philosophers had pursued their various tasks and visions without giving much attention to the question of the nature of philosophy itself. In the wake of German and British idealism, the young philosophers of the present age felt constrained to focus their attention on the values and limits of philosophy. They wanted to become clear about what philosophy is before they continued philosophising.

The concern to analyse philosophy itself naturally led to a concern with the nature of the medium of philosophy, namely language. Analytic philosophers were convinced that many of the confusions inherent in the history of philosophy were the result of playing fast and loose with language. Bertrand Russell and G. E. Moore stand out as British thinkers who most clearly exemplify this early analytic concern. Moore was especially concerned to keep philosophers from soaring to lofty, metaphysical heights by means of their abuse of language, and so he insisted on asking for the common-sense meaning of philosophical terminology. His writings clearly portray this analytic concern for language.[3] Russell went further in his efforts to clarify the relationship between language and philosophy. He strove to demonstrate that the task of philosophy is that of analysing language so as to lay bare the truth about the way things are. His writings stand as monumental examples of analytic philosophy.[4]

This concern for the analysis of language and philosophy found its European expression in the work of the 'Vienna Circle'. Moritz Schlick had gathered a group of philosophers around himself at the University of Vienna, and their primary concern was to enable philosophy to make the same sort of progress that had been made by the natural sciences. Unsurprisingly, the result of such an approach was the tendency to reduce philosophy to the philosophy of science, including mathematics and logic. Such influential philosophers of science as Herbert Feigl, Rudolph Carnap, and Hans Reichenbach owe much to Schlick and the early days of the Vienna Circle. Although he did not participate in the actual meetings of the circle, the young Ludwig Wittgenstein strongly influenced, and was influenced by, the main themes of what has been designated 'Logical Positivism'. Indeed, his *Tractatus Logico-Philosophicus*[5] is often considered the manifesto of this movement.[6]

In the English-speaking world the clearest and most influential expression of this approach to philosophy is found in A. J. Ayer's *Language, Truth and Logic*. The basic thrust of Ayer's book is fairly simple to understand, but its implications are exceedingly revolutionary. Ayer operates on the assumption, which he later explicates, that there are only two types of language which can be said to admit to knowledge and truth, namely logical discourse and empirical assertions. Logical statements can be said to yield knowledge and truth by definition. Given a certain set of definitions and procedural rules, one can determine whether or not a certain statement is consistent with those definitions and rules. If it is, then the statement can be said to be 'true' or 'tautological'. If it is not consistent, then the statement is said to be 'contradictory'. Accordingly, such statements as '2+2 = 4' and 'all brothers are males' are true tautologically, while '3+2 = 7' and 'all quadrupeds have five legs' are contradictory. Empirical statements admit to truth claims on the basis of empirical verification. Every empirical statement makes predictions about future experience, and if these predictions are fulfilled, then the statement is 'true'. If the predictions are not fulfilled, then the statement is 'false'. For example, the statement 'it is raining outside' is true if one can see rain falling, gets wet upon going outside, etc. If these conditions are not met, then the statement is 'false'. Thus there are only these two senses of truth, the logical and the empirical.

With this conception of truth in mind, Ayer argues that, since philosophy is concerned only with the question of truth, it must limit its focus to statements of a logical or empirical nature. All other statements, such as directives, exclamations, and interrogations, lie outside the area of philosophical concern. Since truth has to do with cognition, only logical and empirical discourse can be said to be cognitively significant, or meaningful. Those uses of language which provide no logical nor empirical criteria for truth are rendered cognitively meaningless or, to use Ayer's term, 'nonsense'.

The above considerations are summarised by Ayer in the 'verifiability criterion of meaning'. Ayer says:

'The criterion which we use to test the genuineness of apparent statements of fact is the criterion of verifiability. We say that a sentence is factually significant to any given person, if, and only if, he knows how to verify the proposition which it purports to express—that is, if he knows what observations would lead him,

19

under certain conditions, to accept the proposition as being true, or reject it as being false.'[7]

The effect of such a criterion for meaningfulness on traditional philosophy was obviously devastating. Both ethics and metaphysics were eliminated by Ayer from the realm of meaningful philosophical discourse, since the former uses language to direct action while the latter uses it to express emotion. At best, metaphysics becomes an interesting study in creative picture-thinking. The deep puzzles of classical metaphysics are seen to be pseudo-problems which have arisen because philosophers have been confused about the functions of language. Since theology has invariably been classified as a type of metaphysics, it shares the same fate. Because it purports to discuss and describe a reality that is beyond experience, theological discourse is beyond verification, and is therefore to be classified as 'cognitively meaningless'.

A rather extensive quotation from Ayer is the best way to indicate precisely what results when the verifiability criterion for meaning is applied to theological language.

'It is now generally admitted, at any rate by philosophers, that the existence of a being having the attributes which define the god of any non-animistic religion cannot be demonstratively proved. To see that this is so, we have only to ask ourselves what are the premises from which the existence of such a god could be deduced. If the conclusion that a god exists is to be demonstratively certain, then these premises must be certain; for, as the conclusion of a deductive argument is already contained in the premises, any uncertainty there may be about the truth of the premises is necessarily shared by it. But we know that no empirical proposition can ever be anything more than probable. It is only *a priori* propositions that are logically certain. But we cannot deduce the existence of a god from an *a priori* proposition. For we know that the reason why *a priori* propositions are certain is that they are tautologies. And from a set of tautologies nothing but a further tautology can be validly deduced. It follows that there is no possibility of demonstrating the existence of a god.

'What is not so generally recognised is that there can be no way of proving that the existence of a god, such as the God of Christianity, is even probable. Yet this also is easily shown. For if the existence of such a god were probable, then the proposition that he existed would be an empirical hypothesis. And in that case it would be possible to deduce from it, and other empirical hypotheses, certain experiential propositions which were not deducible from those other hypotheses alone. But in fact this is not possible. It is sometimes claimed, indeed, that the existence of a certain sort of regularity in nature constitutes sufficient evidence for the existence of a god. But if the sentence "God exists" entails no more than that certain types of phenomena occur in certain sequences, then to assert the existence of a god will be simply equivalent to asserting that there is the requisite regularity in nature; and no religious man would admit that this was all he intended to assert in asserting the existence of a god. He would say that in talking about God, he was talking about a transcendent being who might be known through certain empirical manifestations, but certainly could not be defined in terms of those manifestations. But in that case the term "god" is a metaphysical term. And if "god" is a metaphysical term, then it cannot be even probable that a god exists. For to say that "God exists" is to make a metaphysical utterance which cannot be either true or false. And by the same criterion, no sentence which purports to describe the nature of a transcendent god can possess any literal significance.[8]

The challenge that this early, positivistic phase of logical empiricism presented to the users of religious language can be summarised in a variety of ways. One way is by means of a syllogism which, although it tends to oversimplify, has the advantage of pointedness. Moreover, such a syllogistic statement of the challenge serves to distinguish the various responses to it quite clearly, and thereby provides a bridge between the present chapter and the next. The following syllogism is offered as a helpful summary of the initial argument of logical empiricism with respect to religious language:

All cognitively meaningful language is either definitional or empirical.
No religious language is either definitional or empirical.
Therefore, no religious language is cognitively meaningful language.

2 THE LOGICAL EMPIRICIST PHASE

It was not long before a whole host of criticisms of Ayer's original position began to appear, thus necessitating several serious modifications in the logical empiricist challenge. This is often referred to as the 'second phase' of the movement. Almost immediately, it became clear that the verifiability criterion would have to be made more precise. The concept of 'logical possibility' was incorporated in order to avoid the vagueness inherent in the requirement that a statement is only meaningful if it is possible to verify it. Clearly, technical and physical limitations connected with the verification of a particular statement do not render it cognitively meaningless. In addition, 'confirmation' was substituted for 'verification' in order to provide for the cognitive significance of statements about past and future events, which might never be verified in the strict sense of that term.

Another, and more serious, criticism was raised in connection with the status of the verifiability criterion itself. Just how is the statement which expresses this criterion to be classified? It would seem that it must either be a definition, in which case it is essentially arbitrary, or an empirical report (or prediction), in which case it is not at all clear how it could be verified. In fact, it could even be maintained that, far from eliminating metaphysical statements, this criterion is itself the expression of a metaphysical point of view, since it implies certain assertions about the way in which reality is to be viewed. At the very best, such a criterion of meaning might be adequate for the physical sciences, but it would hardly function for other dimensions of human discourse.

In view of such difficulties, the verification principle came in for further modification. Ayer himself included a twenty-two page introduction in the second edition (1946) of his book, in which he sought to re-work his position in light of criticisms which had been developed over the ten intervening years. Therein he states that he now holds the verifiability criterion in the 'weak', or 'logically confirmable' sense,[9] and that he views it as a non-arbitrary definition which can be justified pragmatically.[10] Ayer goes on to acknowledge that there might be another criterion of meaning which could be adopted for various reasons, but 'Nevertheless, I think that, unless it satisfied the principle of verification, it would not be capable of being understood in the sense in which either scientific hypotheses or common-sense statements are habitually understood'.[11] Overlooking the highly questionable nature of this view of 'common-sense statements', it can be seen that Ayer's later position is much more tolerant than his early one. And yet, Ayer never actually addresses himself to the implications of this later view for the language of theology.

Another manifestation of the more tolerant phase of logical empiricism which bears more directly on the question of religious and theological language is found in the writings of such thinkers as John Wisdom and Anthony Flew. The most salient characteristic of this aspect of the movement is the willingness to discuss seriously the question of religious discourse, and even, in the case of Wisdom, the tendency to view such language as having its own distinct logic. The purpose is not to demonstrate that religious language is meaningless, but to explore it with an eye to the possibility of its having its own unique function. John Wisdom's 'garden parable', found in his discussion entitled 'Gods',[12] provides the setting for much of the more recent debate.

'Two people return to their long neglected garden and find among the weeds a few of the old plants surprisingly vigorous. One says to the other "It must be that a gardener has been coming and doing something about these plants". Upon inquiry they find that no neighbour has ever seen anyone at work in their garden. The first man says to the other "He must have worked while people slept". The other says "No, someone would have heard him and besides, anybody who cared about the plants would have kept down these weeds". The first man says "Look at the way these are arranged. There is purpose and a feeling for beauty here. I believe that someone comes, someone invisible to mortal eyes. I believe that the more carefully we look the more we shall find confirmation of this." They examine the garden ever so carefully and sometimes they come on new things suggesting that a gardener comes and sometimes they come on new things suggesting the contrary and even that a malicious person has been at work. Besides examining the garden carefully they also study what happens to gardens left without attention. Each learns all the other learns about this and about the garden. Consequently, when after all this, one says, "I still believe a gardener comes" while the other says "I don't" their different words now reflect no difference as to what they have found in the garden, no difference as to what they would find in the garden if they looked further and no difference about how fast untended gardens fall into disorder. At this stage, in this context, the gardener hypothesis has ceased to be experimental, the difference between one who accepts and one who rejects it is now not a matter of the one expecting something the other does not expect. What is the difference between them? The one says

23

"A gardener comes unseen and unheard. He is manifested only in his works with which we are all familiar," the other says "There is no gardener" and with this difference in what they say about the gardener goes a difference in how they feel towards the garden, in spite of the fact that neither expects anything of it which the other does not expect.'[13]

Wisdom goes on to conclude that judgements about the existence of God are similar to judgements about aesthetic experience, in that they are more than emotive expressions, but less than factual judgements. Religious discussions, along with aesthetic controversies, have their own procedures for settlement.[14] Although Wisdom does not engage in any analysis of such procedures, his approach contributed to a whole new discussion among philosophers and theologians.

The volume which best expresses the initial concerns of this new discussion was brought together by Anthony Flew and Alasdair MacIntyre.[15] Since that time several other volumes of discussion have been published which continue to explore the nature of religious language.[16] Clearly, the discussion is far from being concluded. Although the Flew and MacIntyre volume contains a number of contributions and emphases, it is perhaps not unfair to suggest that its dominant drive is best expressed by the contribution of Anthony Flew himself. Moreover, it is Flew who characterises the mood of the modified challenge of logical empiricism.

Against the backdrop of Wisdom's 'garden parable' Flew dramatises the dilemma of religious language. At the outset, statements about God are patterned after regular empirical assertions, but in the face of contrary evidence they are systematically qualified in such a way as to render them void of meaning. 'A fine brash hypothesis may thus be killed by inches, the death by a thousand qualifications.'[17] Since the crucial factor in such a transformation is the confrontation with contrary evidence, Flew goes on to conclude that there is something suspicious about religious language because it systematically absorbs all attempts to falsify it. In this way he constructs what has been called the 'principle of falsification' as a standard for cognitive meaning.

'Now to assert that such and such is the case is necessarily equivalent to denying that such and such is not the case. Suppose then that we are in doubt as to what someone who gives vent to an utterance is asserting, or suppose that, more radically, we are sceptical as to whether he is really asserting anything at all, one way of trying to understand (or perhaps it will be to expose) his utterance is to attempt to find what he would regard as counting against, or as being incompatible with, its truth. For if the utterance is indeed an assertion, it will necessarily be equivalent to a denial of the negation of that assertion. Anything which would count against the assertion, or which would induce the speaker to withdraw it and to admit that it had been mistaken, must be part of (or the whole of) the meaning of the negation of that assertion. And to know the meaning of the negation of an assertion, is as near as makes no matter, to know the meaning of that assertion. And if there is nothing which a putative assertion denies then there is nothing which it asserts either; and so it is not really an assertion. When the Sceptic in the parable asked the Believer, "Just how does what you call an invisible, intangible, eternally elusive gardener differ from an imaginary gardener or even from no gardener at all?" he was suggesting that the Believer's earlier statement had been so eroded by qualification that it was no longer an assertion at all.'[18]

Although Flew's 'falsification criterion of meaning' is stated more tolerantly than was Ayer's verifiability criterion, the difference between the two is slight. In terms of the syllogism used to summarise Ayer's challenge, Flew's major and minor premises appear to be different from Ayer's. Actually, however, they are logically equivalent, since 'falsifiable' is just another way of saying 'definitional or empirical' (verifiable). Here is a syllogistic summary of Flew's challenge:

All cognitively meaningful language is falsifiable in principle.
No religious language is falsifiable in principle.
Therefore, no religious language is cognitively meaningful language.

So it can be seen that although the second, modified phase of logical empiricism is more willing to discuss the question of religious language, the challenge to the users of such language remains essentially the same.

3   THE LINGUISTIC ANALYSIS PHASE[19]

It is possible to maintain that logical empiricism has entered into a third phase, often termed 'language philosophy' or 'linguistic analysis'. Setting aside for the moment the question of historical development, it is the case that a great number of philosophers today consider themselves participants in the activity so designated. Moreover, this new emphasis on the analysis of language has added a good deal of vigour to the discussion concerning religious discourse. Although there are several outstanding thinkers who exemplify this approach, nearly all owe their initial inspiration to the work of the later Ludwig Wittgenstein. For this reason it will be of help to present a summary of Wittgenstein's later philosophy by way of pointing up the implications of this approach for the discussion concerning religious language. The following sketch of Wittgenstein's thought should make it clear that, although language philosophy grew out of the issues raised by logical empiricism, at its core it represents an approach which is often diametrically opposed to that of Ayer, Flew, and even the early Wittgenstein!

Wittgenstein conceived of the function and purpose of philosophy as the analysis of language. This accounts for a good deal of the significance of the title of his last writings, *Philosophical Investigations*. In his own words:

> 'Our investigation is therefore a grammatical one. Such an investigation sheds light on our problem by clearing misunderstandings away. Misunderstandings concerning the use of words, caused, among other things, by certain analogies between the forms of expression in different regions of language.—Some of them can be removed by substituting one form of expression for another; this may be called an "analysis" of our forms of expression, for the process is sometimes like one of taking a thing apart.'[20]

The reason for stressing the analysis of language as the essence of philosophy is really quite simple. Wittgenstein did not think that the problem of understanding experience has its source in the nature of experience. The problem has its source in our attempt to understand (conceptualise) and communicate our experience. He thought that we would understand and communicate our own experience and the experience of others better if we paid more attention to the ways in which we talk about such experiences.

For Wittgenstein, the uses and functions of language were the beginning points for understanding. These uses and functions form the very structure of experiences and daily living, and thus Wittgenstein conceived of them as 'the given' or 'forms of life'.[21] In another passage he refers to the various rules for the use of language as 'bedrock' and thus beyond any sort of ultimate justification.[22]

One of the unique characteristics of Wittgenstein's approach to philosophy is his conception of philosophical problems as similar to psychological 'diseases' or 'mental cramps'. When one begins to analayse philosophical language, one begins to notice how many philosophical problems are literally produced by a confused and/or negligent extension of ordinary language. The philosopher is one who is worried or anxious about the difficulties and puzzles deriving from his analysis of language. These anxieties or 'illnesses', are 'cured' by the philosopher through a clarification of the mistaken understanding and use of language. 'The philosopher's treatment of a question is like the treatment of an illness.'[23] Thus, in one sense, the philosopher functions as a therapist in relieving his own and others' puzzlements.

There are at least two simple, but fatal, mistakes in the philosophical use of language which Wittgenstein singles out. First, 'A main cause of philosophical disease—a one-sided diet: one nourishes one's thinking with only one kind of example'.[24] Here he would seem to have in mind a tendency among many philosophers to conceive of, or to define, a particular word according to a given pattern or presupposition, and then to conclude that this word or concept must always correspond to this definition. One might suggest the logical positivist's conception of 'meaning' and 'truth' as examples of this 'one-sided diet'.

Secondly, the first passage quoted mentions misunderstandings caused by analogies between the forms of expression. Thus, three sentences may be similar in grammatical form, such as 'The book is red', 'The man is good', and 'The soul is immortal', but dissimilar in logical function. To insist that all sentences of the same form must have the same logic is as naïve as to insist that all currency of the same denomination has the same international value.

The philosopher's function is to cure these basic diseases and problems. Such a cure is effected by analysing the many varieties of language structure and function, and then making precise distinctions among them which will serve as reminders for future use. These various language structures are illuminated by likening them to the structure and rules of games. Wittgenstein's writings are replete with very simple 'language games' which reveal much concerning how and why language functions as it does.

These philosophical problems, which Wittgenstein also referred

Ian Ramsey

to as 'mental cramps', are solved, not only by supplying answers, but by restating and thus elminating the problem.

> 'It is not our aim to refine or complete the system of rules for the use of words in unheard-of-ways.
> 'For the clarity that we are aiming at is indeed *complete* clarity. But this simply means that the philosophical problem could *completely* disappear.
> 'The real discovery is the one that makes me capable of stopping doing philosophy when I want to.—The one that gives philosophy peace, so that it is no longer tormented by questions which bring *itself* in question.—Instead, we now demonstrate a method, by examples; and the series of examples can be broken off.— Problems are solved (difficulties eliminated), not a *single* problem. 'There is not *a* philosophical method, though there are indeed methods, like different therapies.'[25]

Although the analysis of language is an extremely complex activity (and because of the constant growth and change of language, one that will never be completed), there are basic guidelines which Wittgenstein suggested. One is that the meaning of a word or sentence is defined in terms of its use. This principle is embodied in the most often-quoted motto of Wittgenstein's followers, 'Don't ask for meaning, ask for use'. In Wittgenstein's own words:

> 'One cannot guess how a word functions. One has to *look at* its use and learn from that.
> 'But the difficulty is to remove the prejudice which stands in the way of doing this. It is not a *stupid* prejudice.'[26]

This principle is consonant with Wittgenstein's concept of words being like chess pieces, each being defined in terms of its function. 'The question "What is a word really?" is analogous to "What is a piece in chess?" '[27] The idea here is just that, as one answers the question 'What is a knight?' by explaining and showing the ways in which a knight may and may not be moved, so one answers the question 'What is knowledge?' by explaining and illustrating how the word 'knowledge' functions. By distinguishing the ways in which the word is used, and the situations in which it is accepted or rejected, one comes to an understanding of what the term means. 'Essence is expressed by grammar.'[28]

Another helpful guideline for the analysis of language which

Wittgenstein suggests, and which is really implied in the above suggestion, is that meaning is determined by the rules of the various, overlapping language 'games' or regions. Each language could be represented as a vast, interrelated network of words and sentences. Each region of this network develops out of, and is tied down to, a specific area or aspect of experience. Each region develops somewhat independently and thus has its own rules, or grammar. There are, however, many similarities or 'family-resemblances' among their individual grammars. The philosopher must be careful not to be misled by these similarities into thinking that they all operate in the same way. At the same time, these grammars do have things in common, especially their grounding in experience, and these need to be kept in mind also. These grammars, rules, or 'forms of life' are the final justification for our particular conceptualisations and communications:

' "How am I able to obey a rule?"—if this is not a question about causes, then it is about the justification for my following the rule in the way I do.
'If I have exhausted the justification I have reached bedrock, and my spade is turned. Then I am inclined to say: "This is simply what I do".'[29]

A corollary to the above stated principle is that no one set of rules has universal priority. That is to say, one cannot insist on applying the rules of one region of language in all regions. This would be similar to insisting on applying the rules of English grammar to all other languages. There simply is no aristocracy or hierarchy of language functions and rules, hence there is none for meanings either. What may be 'meaningless' within one language structure may be very meaningful within another, depending on the purpose and grammar of the individual sentence in question. As Wittgenstein himself says:

'To say: "This combination of words makes no sense" excludes it from the sphere of language and thereby bounds the domain of language. But when one draws a boundary it may be for various kinds of reasons. If I surround an area with a fence or a line or otherwise, the purpose may be to prevent someone from getting in or out; but it may also be a part of a game and the players be supposed, say, to jump over the boundary; or it may shew where the property of one man ends and that of another begins; and so on. So if I draw a boundary line that is not yet to say what I am drawing it for.

'When a sentence is called senseless, it is not as it were its sense that is senseless. But a combination of words is being excluded from the language, withdrawn from circulation.'[30]

The equality of language structures would seem, according to Wittgenstein, to apply even to the claim of formal logic for purity and rigour.[31] The passage cited is not altogether clear in its implications, but it does seem to imply that formal logic is not the best method of communication for all situations. The same can be said, to a lesser degree, of the principle of induction.[32] The ultimate justification which can be given for any standard of meaning and truth within a language structure is a pragmatic one. One goal of language is the communication of information, and thus both formal consistency and material correspondence are necessary to this end. However, there may be other functions of language as well, and indeed there are, which necessitate different standards. Commands, questions, rituals, and poetry are all important and depend upon other standards for achieving their purpose.[33]

One other outworking of this approach bears mentioning. It would seem that, according to Wittgenstein's approach, truth, as well as meaning, is determined by use. Agreement in the use of a statement within a 'region' of language, or according to 'forms of life', becomes the standard of truth. Thus truth will vary in accord with the different purposes and functions of language.[34]

' "So you are saying that human agreement decides what is true and what is false?"—It is what human beings *say* that is true and false; and they agree in the *language* they use. That is not agreement in opinions but in form of life.

'If language is to be a means of communication there must be agreement not only in definitions but also (queer as this may sound) in judgements. This seems to abolish logic, but does not do so.—It is one thing to describe methods of measurement, and another to obtain and state results of measurement. But what we call "measuring" is partly determined by a certain constancy in results of measurements.'[35]

I have discussed Wittgenstein's views on philosophy and language at length partly because I am convinced that it is essential to see the differences between his approach and that of logical empiricism, and partly because in many ways the views of Ian Ramsey, the late Bishop of Durham, are based on the insights of Wittgenstein. In other words, Bishop Ramsey makes use of Wittgenstein's method by way of meeting the challenge of logical empiricism. There is a sense in which John Wisdom, who was a student of Wittgenstein's, can be said to suggest a Wittgensteinian approach to religious language, but it is also clear that Wisdom did little more than keep open the door to further discussion. It is Ramsey who makes a serious attempt to carry out the analysis of religious language in some detail.

There are also other philosophers who have developed important insights into the nature of language after the manner of Wittgenstein, and the influence of these insights on Ramsey's thought will become apparent later on. Such thinkers as Gilbert Ryle, Max Black, and John Austin[36] are especially important in this connection. This is not to say that these thinkers actually address themselves to the problem of religious language, but only that their works are replete with insights which have direct bearing on the topic in question. In like manner, Ramsey's use of such insights is far more in terms of method than in terms of actual content.

Although the revolutionary insights of the later Wittgenstein and his followers hover in the background, the major responses to logical empiricism by religious thinkers have been fashioned in reply to the challenge as summarised in the syllogisms presented earlier. In fact, there is a sense in which one could maintain that much of the discussion about religious language goes on as if neither the philosophers nor the theologians involved had ever really read Wittgenstein! For this reason the next chaper will be devoted to tracing the logic of these responses in light of the arguments of logical empiricism proper.

NOTES

1 The task of naming contemporary movements is notoriously hazardous, but none the less necessary. The names I have chosen for these phases of logical empiricism reflect American usage.
2 Morton White, *The Age of Analysis*.
3 G. E. Moore, *Philosophical Papers*.
4 Perhaps the most comprehensive presentation of Russell's approach is R. E. Egner and L. E. Denonn (eds), *The Basic Writings of Bertrand Russell*.
5 Translated by D. F. Pears and B. F. McGuiness.
6 One of the best accounts of Logical Positivism is Victor Kraft's *The Vienna Circle*.

7 A. J. Ayer, *Language, Truth and Logic*.
8 ibid., p. 114.
9 ibid., p. 13.
10 ibid., p. 16
11 ibid., p. 16.
12 John Wisdom, *Philosophy and Psycho-Analysis*, pp. 149–59.
13 Quote taken from G. L. Abernethy and T. A. Langford (eds), *Philosophy of Religion*, p. 345.
14 ibid., p. 348.
15 Anthony Flew and Alasdair MacIntyre (eds), *New Essays in Philosophical Theology*.
16 Basil Mitchell (ed.), *Faith and Logic*; Sidney Hook (ed.), *Religious Experience and Truth*; John Hick (ed.), *Faith and the Philosophers*.
17 Flew, 'Theology and Falsification', in Flew & MacIntyre (eds), *New Essays*, p. 97.
18 ibid., p. 98.
19 A major part of this section was first published, in somewhat different form, under the title 'Wittgenstein and Religious Language' in *Theology Today*, XXI, no. 1 (April 1964), p. 59.
20 Ludwig Wittgenstein, *Philosophical Investigations*, trans. G. E. M. Anscombe, p. 43, para. 90b.
21 ibid., p. 226.
22 ibid., p. 85, para. 217.
23 ibid., p. 91, para. 255.
24 ibid., p. 155, para. 593.
25 ibid., p. 51, para. 133.
26 ibid., p. 109, para. 340.
27 ibid., p. 47, para. 108d.
28 ibid., p. 116, para. 371.
29 ibid., p. 85, para. 217.
30 ibid., pp. 138–9, paras 499–500.
31 ibid., p. 46, paras 107–8.
32 ibid., p. 136, paras 481–2.
33 ibid., pp. 11–12, para. 23.
34 ibid., p. 86, para. 224.
35 ibid., p. 88, paras 241–2.
36 Gilbert Ryle, *The Concept of Mind* and *Dilemmas*; Max Black, *Models and Metaphors*; John L. Austin, *Philosophical Papers* and *How To Do Things With Words*.

Chapter 2

THE RESPONSE OF PHILOSOPHICAL THEOLOGY[1]

Many of the various responses to the challenge of logical empiricism, which have been developed by thinkers concerned with philosophical theology, may be classified roughly according to a threefold division. First, there are those who accept the argument in its entirety, but do not think that the conclusion that religious language is cognitively meaningless is at all detrimental to religion. Second, there are those who refuse to accept the conclusion of the argument because they are not prepared to accept its major premise that all cognitively significant language must either be definitional or empirical. Third, there are those who refuse to accept the conclusion because they reject the minor premise that no religious language is empirical in nature. Clearly, such a classification of the responses is oversimplified, but it will provide a schema for presenting the different emphases of those who have written on the subject. Obviously, there will be some writers who will go unmentioned, but a sufficient number will be included to provide a background against which to see Ian Ramsey's position in adequate perspective. Nothing will be said concerning those thinkers who accept the argument of logical empiricism as it stands, since according to them nothing more remains to be said.

1 COMPLETE ACCEPTANCE

Some thinkers, by training and vocation often more philosophical than theological, respond to the foregoing argument by accepting the truth of both of the premises and of the conclusion as well. These thinkers differ, however, from those who go on to say that

B

religious language is nonsensical. They maintain that even though religious language is not cognitively meaningful, it is very significant from an emotional, ethical, or existential point of view. That is to say, once we get straight about the true nature of religious language, the challenge of logical empiricism is no longer devastating to the use of such language.

Two very prominent British philosophers have expressed this point of view, namely R. M. Hare and R. B. Braithwaite. Hare develops his view of religious belief as an unverifiable and unfalsifiable interpretation of one's experience in his contribution to *New Essays in Philosophical Theology*.[2] He suggests that religious beliefs are really principles of interpretation, or frames of reference, by means of which one interprets his experience. As such, religious beliefs are not subject to true and false judgements, because they simply do not assert any state of affairs. Hare calls such beliefs 'bliks' and likens them to the perspective of a paranoid who is convinced that all Oxford dons are out to do him in. Thus there is no factual disagreement between the two statements 'God exists' and 'God does not exist'. The real difference is one of perspective—like the difference between optimism and pessimism.

> 'Suppose we believe that everything that happened, happened by pure chance. This would not of course be an assertion; for it is compatible with anything happening or not happening, and so, incidentally, is its contradictory. But if we had this belief, we would not be able to explain or predict or plan anything. Thus, although we should not be asserting anything different from those of a more normal belief, there would be a great difference between us; and this is the sort of difference that there is between those who really believe in God and those who really disbelieve in him.'[3]

It is clear that if religious beliefs are viewed as bliks, then the language in which these beliefs are expressed is neither empirical nor definitional in nature. Thus Hare in effect accepts the argument of logical empiricism but endeavours to redefine the nature and function of religious beliefs and language.

R. B. Braithwaite also redefines the nature of religious language by likening it to the language of morality and commendation. When a person expresses a religious statement, he is not asserting a fact but indicating a commitment to, and commendation of, a certain attitude or policy of action. In his own words: 'A religious

assertion, for me, is the assertion of an intention to carry out a
certain behaviour policy, subsumable under a sufficiently general
principle to be a moral one, together with the implicit or explicit
statement, but not the assertion of certain stories.'[4] In other words,
Braithwaite, like Hare, concurs with the argument of logical
empiricism that religious language is not cognitively meaningful, but
he does not think that this renders religious language ethically
meaningless.

Another thinker whose thought fits into this general category is
Paul Tillich. In the section of his *Systematic Theology* entitled 'The
Reality of God', Tillich takes up the question of the possibility of
knowledge of God. This, in turn, raises the problem of religious
language. He wastes no time in clearly stating his position: 'The
statement that God is being-itself is a nonsymbolic statement. It
does not point beyond itself. It means what it says directly and
properly. . . . However, after this has been said, nothing else can
be said about God as God which is not symbolic.'[5]

This position, that all language about God except the statement
'God is being-itself' is symbolic, is based on a distinction between
'sign' and 'symbol'. A sign, for Tillich, has an arbitrary relation
to that to which it points (e.g., a table could be designated by a sign
other than 'table', if people were to so stipulate), while a symbol
'participates in the reality for which it stands'.[6] The term 'God' is
said to 'participate in the power of the divine to which it points',
rather than designate some being within the totality of reality.

'There can be no doubt that any concrete assertion about God
must be symbolic, for a concrete assertion is one which uses a
segment of finite experience in order to say something about him.
It transcends the content of this segment, although it also includes
it. The segment of finite reality which becomes the vehicle of a
concrete assertion about God is affirmed and negated at the same
time. It becomes a symbol, for a symbolic expression is one whose
proper meaning is negated by that to which it points. And yet it
also is affirmed by it, and this affirmation gives the symbolic
expression an adequate basis for pointing beyond itself.'[7]

In response to the question of how a symbol derived from finite
experience can function as a symbol of that which is infinite,
Tillich maintains that only when God is viewed as being-itself can
the concept of God-talk as analogical be accepted. If God is viewed
as another being among beings, then it is impossible to bridge the

gap between the finite and the infinite; but if God is seen as being-itself, then all statements about the finite become statements about the infinite, and vice versa.

'If a segment of reality is used as a symbol for God, the realm of reality from which it is taken is, so to speak, elevated into the realm of the holy. It no longer is secular. It is theonomous. If God is called the "king", something is said not only about God but also about the holy character of kinghood. If God's work is called "making whole" or "healing", this not only says something about God but also emphasises the theonomous character of all healing. If God's self-manifestation is called "the word", this not only symbolises God's relation to man but also emphasises the holiness of all words as an expression of the spirit.'[8]

Tillich faces the question of the truth of such religious symbols in an oblique manner. He says:

'A religious symbol possesses some truth if it adequately expresses the correlation of revelation in which some person stands. A religious symbol *is* true if it adequately expresses the correlation of some person with final revelation. . . . The judgement that a religious symbol *is* true is identical with the judgement that the revelation of which it is the adequate expression is true. This double meaning of the truth of a symbol must be kept in mind. A symbol *has* truth: it is adequate to the revelation it expresses. A symbol *is* true: it is the expression of a true revelation.'[9]

Although Tillich seems to hedge on this matter in his *Dynamics of Faith*, in that he avoids saying anything about the possibility or necessity of a non-symbolic statement about God, his most recent statements on this subject confirm his earlier position. In a symposium, *Religious Experience and Truth*, Tillich says:

'But the word "God" involves a double meaning: it connotes the unconditioned transcendent, the ultimate, and also an object somehow endowed with qualities and actions. The first is not figurative or symbolic, but is rather in the strictest sense what it is said to be. The second, however, is really symbolic, figurative.'[10]

Thus he continues to maintain that the statement about God as being-itself is non-symbolic, even though he neglects to indicate how this statement is to be verified.

On the other hand, a case could be made for classifying Tillich's view of religious language as a form of the position which denies the major premise of the empiricist argument. 'God is being-itself', as non-symbolic, would presumably be true. It is also true that Tillich often asserts that religious statements are none the less true for being symbolic. In other words, he does seem to claim that there are forms of cognitive truth other than the logical and the empirical.[11] And yet, although he claims to set forth the criteria of such truth,[12] it is very difficult to determine whether or not he has actually done so. I have classified Tillich's view along with those of Hare and Braithwaite because I think that, in the final analysis, Tillich's emphasis on the symbolic function of religious language overrides his concern for cognitive truth. This is borne out by the fact that John H. Randall's interpretation of religious discourse as symbolic, which is admitted by both Randall and Tillich to be essentially similar to Tillich's, gives hardly any place to the cognitive function of God-talk.[13]

By way of pointing up difficulties, at least three things can be said about this approach. First, it does not seem to be in harmony with the way religious language is used. Most religious people would object if you told them that their religious beliefs are neither true nor false. Second, it raises the question as to how one chooses between right and wrong bliks, and/or ethical commitments. Unfortunately, neither Hare nor Braithwaite faces up to this question. Third, many would maintain that the teachings of Christ were meant as assertions about human experience that can be confirmed or disconfirmed. Even Tillich's symbolic interpretation leaves much to be desired on all of these points. As will be seen in Part Two, frequent objectors notwithstanding, Ramsey's position has less in common with this approach than with either of the following two approaches.

2   COMPLETE REJECTION

Other thinkers are not prepared to accept the argument offered by logical empiricism. Some of these, by training and vocation usually more theological than philosophical, respond to the challenge by rejecting the truth of the major premise. The main contention of those taking this approach is that cognitive meaning cannot be confined to the logical and empirical realm. Here it is maintained that religious truth, along with other forms of metaphysical truth, is a form of cognition that has a unique nature. Since such truth is embodied in religious language, religious language may be cognitively meaningful even though it is neither logical nor empirical in nature.

One of the most articulate exponents of the point of view that rejects the first premise is Michael Foster.[14] Foster identifies revelation, and thus the religious language that expresses revelation, with mystery. He objects to the logical empiricists' demand for clarity in our talk about experience. Thus he would conclude that revelation can be cognitively meaningful, that is, subject to the judgement 'true', without being reducible to either logical or empirical language. Foster says:

> 'Revelation is of mystery, but mystery revealed is not eliminated, but remains mysterious. It remains an object of wonder, which is dispelled when mystery is eliminated. There is no method by which revelation can be commanded: "it is" (in the Bible) "not a thing to be procured from God by any technique". That is to to say, it is not subject to human mastery.'[15]

Although the first sentence in this quotation raises many other questions, there can be no question that Foster rejects the major premise of the logical empiricist argument.

Willem Zuurdeeg also refuses to accept the statement that all cognitively meaningful statements are either logical or empirical in nature. Zuurdeeg is concerned to stress the convictional nature of religious language. Its primary function is the expression of ultimate convictions.[16] He maintains that religious truth, and thus religious language, is unique in that it is not limited to propositional assertions. Moreover, it cannot be analysed or justified. Nevertheless, Zuurdeeg wants to maintain that such statements are still meaningful and true.

> 'I must protest vehemently against the notion that language of Christian faith consists of propositions which can be analysed by means of logic. If it does not make sense to a philosopher to attempt a logical analysis of persons, how much sense will it make to a theologian to try to do so with the Lord God? Exactly in the way that man is man-who-speaks, so God is God-who-speaks. Can we offer a logical analysis of the Creator of Heaven and Earth? Shall we discard the doctrine of the Trinity simply because the language in which it is expressed is logically inconsistent?'[17]

Another thinker whose view is closely related to those of Foster and Zuurdeeg is William Hordern.[18] Chapters five and six of his book, *Speaking of God,* set forth the premises of Hordern's position. The first premise maintains, following Wittgenstein, that all language is to be understood as a vast and complex group of internally autonomous but overlapping 'language games'. The standards of meaning and truth vary from one such 'game' (e.g. physical science) to another (e.g. religion). The second premise asserts, following Zuurdeeg, that religious language is to be understood as essentially 'convictional' in nature. That is, religious language expresses a commitment to a certain way of life which is not the result of a rational process, but is rather the framework within which theological reasoning takes place. Hordern devotes a good deal of space to showing that all knowledge claims are only meaningful and confirmable within a given context, and this context itself cannot be justified in terms of its own criteria. The conclusion which Hordern draws from these two premises is that Christian language can be shown to be meaningful when it is viewed as an autonomous language game which is based in the experience of the Christian community. Incidentally, Hordern openly acknowledges the similarities between his own view and R. M. Hare's 'blik' approach.

'We can locate the logic of faith if we note that, as Wittgenstein says, the giving of reasons must come to an end. When a particular belief is challenged we can give reasons for it. But when we have given all the reasons we can, when we have made all the moves possible in the language game, no more can be done. If someone does not play the game, no further reasoning can force him to do so.'[19]

Despite the fact that the approach represented here seems to argue on the side of angels, there are several difficulties that arise in connection with it. First, it runs the risk of rendering religious language so distinct from all other language that it becomes irrelevant. Second, no extra-logical criteria are offered by means of which one can even decipher the content of religious statements, let alone distinguish between those that are true and those that are not. Third, few would contest the belief that reality and experience cannot be completely represented in language, but this should not be used to licence sloppy talk. Fourth, whether or not revelation is true is not the real problem; rather, the problem is which statements are to be taken as revelation. Some would maintain that the best way to honour revelation and mystery is to apply rigid standards so as to be able to distinguish non-sense and falsehood from meaning and truth. Finally, this approach ignores the fact that the 'religious language-game' overlaps with many other language games and cannot be sharply distinguished from them. Although his views are often accused of being insular in precisely this way, it will become clear upon examination that Ramsey is especially sensitive to the interrelatedness of the various functions of language.

3 QUALIFIED ACCEPTANCE

Another way of responding to the argument of logical empiricism is to accept the major premise, while rejecting the minor premise, and there are those thinkers who have taken up the responsibility of constructing such an approach. The main drive of this approach is found in the attempt to relate religious language to experience and thereby to establish it as cognitively meaningful. The thesis of this approach is that religious language very often fulfils empirical functions and is, therefore, at those times cognitively meaningful. The main burden of such an approach is to specify the exact situations in which religious language can be said to be empirical.

Much of the impetus for this approach can be traced to Basil Mitchell's contribution to the *New Essays in Philosophical Theology* volume. In response to Wisdom's garden parable, Mitchell offers an alternative parable which is aimed at meeting the charges made by Flew and Hare. Mitchell tells the story of a stranger who, although believed to be the leader of the resistance movement by one of its partisan members, appears at times to be in league with the enemy occupational forces. Now, the point of the story is that although this belief concerning the patriotism of the stranger is a factual belief against which evidence can be said to count, no evidence can ever be said to count decisively against this belief. The partisan has such strong personal reasons and evidence for believing in the stranger that no external factors can persuade him otherwise.

'It is here that my parable differs from Hare's. The partisan admits that many things may and do count against his belief: Whereas Hare's lunatic who has a *blik* about dons doesn't admit that anything counts against his *blik*. Also, the partisan has a reason for having in the first instance committed himself, viz. the character of the Stranger'.[20]

Mitchell goes on to indicate that after the war the partisan's belief will be open to empirical confirmation or disconfirmation. This 'after the war' theme is picked up quite pointedly by the next thinker to be considered. Other elements of Mitchell's view will be reflected in the thought of other thinkers yet to be discussed, including Ian Ramsey.

One of the more interesting presentations of the cognitive status of religious language is to be found in the writings of John Hick.[21] Hick maintains that statements that make predictions about experiences taking place after death are open to verification (or at least confirmation). Such verification is termed 'eschatological' by Hick, and, in his view, firmly establishes the cognitive meaningfulness of this type of statement. Space will not permit a full analysis of Hick's views at this juncture. It is sufficient to note that they are explained and presented by one who is fully aware of the challenge of logical empiricism and who endeavours to learn from its insights. Concerning the claim that there will be experiences after death, Hick says:

'The logical peculiarity of the claim is that it is open to confirmation but not to refutation. There can be conclusive evidence for it if it be true, but there cannot be conclusive evidence against it if it be untrue. For if we survive bodily death we shall (presumably) know that we have survived it, but if we do not survive death we shall not know that we have not survived it. The verification situation is thus asymmetrical. However, the religious doctrine at least is open to verification and is accordingly meaningful. Its eschatological prediction assures its status as an assertion.'[22]

Another recent explication of the empirical nature of religious language is found in John Hutchison's *Language and Faith*.[23] Hutchison maintains that since religion is to be understood primarily as a means of comprehensive life orientation, the language of religion is to be understood as the expression and description of various orientations to life. He contends that, like poetry, religious language is very often intended to communicate certain feelings, values, facts, and interpretations of human experience.

It should be clear that such theories or interpretations of life are subject to true and false judgements in the same sense that broad theories about the physical universe are—namely, in terms of confirmation and fruitlessness. In Chapter Five of his book, Hutchison uses the term 'adequacy' to designate the standard by means of which life-orientational theories are to be evaluated. This adequacy implies, in addition to rational consistency and coherence, the standards of sufficient reason, simplicity, empiricism, and critical rigour.[24] As will shortly be seen, these are criteria with which Ramsey is also concerned.

Other writers suggest that much of religious language functions as an empirical-theoretic model. A helpful development of religious language in terms of models can be found in the writings of Frederick Ferré.[25] He outlines the functions of theological models in the following ways:

'Theological speech projects a model of immense responsive significance, drawn from "the facts", as the key to its conceptual synthesis. This model, for theism, is made up of the "spiritual" characteristics of personality: will, purpose, wisdom, love, and the like. For Christianity, more specifically, the conceptual model consists in the creative, self-giving, personal love of Jesus Christ. In this model is found the only literal meaning which these terms, like "creative", "personal", and "love", can have in the Christian vocabulary. All the concepts of the Christian are organised and synthesised in relation to this model. The efforts of systematic theology are bent to explicating the consistency and coherence of the synthesis built on this model of "God" as key concept. Christian preaching is devoted to pointing out the applicability of this conceptual synthesis to common experiences of life. And Christian apologetics struggles to show that the synthesis organised around this model is adequate to the unforced interpretation of all experience, including suffering and evil.'[26]

Ferré goes on to point out that since the language, thoughts, and actions that are based on a given conceptual model can be evaluated in terms of their coherence and adequacy in dealing with experience, it is possible to speak of one model as being more appropriate, or more fruitful, than others.[27] This sort of evaluation implies cognitive meaning, since although the criteria and results of such evaluation are difficult to determine, the models are, in theory, confirmable or disconfirmable.

The most frequent criticisms of this empiricist response to the challenge are two. First, such an approach would seem to compromise the uniqueness of religious language by assimilating it to empirical language. Hick's concept of 'eschatological verification', for instance, would seem to imply an exceedingly straightforward view of religious discourse. Second, it is not clear how the criteria offered by this approach can be successfully applied to religious experience and language. Ferré and Hutchison both tend to leave this question up in the air.

Before moving on to a full-scale examination of Ramsey's interpretation of religious language, it will be helpful to introduce his position at this juncture by relating it to the challenge and responses outlined above. I hope such an introduction will provide a transitional bridge between these two introductory chapters and those that will follow.

It is possible to classify Ramsey's position as in one respect similar to that of Mitchell, Hick, Hutchison, and Ferré, in that he is very concerned to maintain the empirical cognitivity of religious discourse. In fact, the subtitle of his main book is 'An Empirical Placing of Theological Phrases'.[28] Moreover, as the following chapters will make clear, Ramsey is extremely forthright in his appreciation of the contributions of logical empiricism. He goes to great length in warning theologians and lay users of religious language that, if their talk is not anchored in empirical experience, it is neither philosophically nor religiously adequate. In this sense Ramsey can be said to respond to the challenge of logical empiricism by agreeing with its concern for empirical experience, but rejecting the minor premise of its argument, namely that no religious language is empirical in nature.

On the other hand, it would do an injustice to the complexity and profundity of Ramsey's view only to mention its empirical emphasis. For Ramsey is also concerned to make some important modifications in connection with the logical empiricist concept of 'empirical'. In this sense, although with important qualifications, he can be classified as one who rejects the major premise of the empiricist argument, namely, that all cognitively meaningful language is either definitional or empirical. Ramsey rejects this premise in that he opts for a broader conception of what constitutes empirical experience than empiricists usually assume. Specifically, he is concerned to establish the empirical nature of much of ordinary language and theoretical science, even though they are not exhaustively described in terms of object-talk. In this way he seeks to reprimand the empiricists for their dogmatic narrowness.

Along with these emphases on empirical experience and a broadened concept of 'empirical', Ramsey endeavours to establish that, although religious language has certain peculiarities, it is no more odd than much of the language of theoretical science and personal relationships. It is in this way that Ramsey can be seen as taking a much more radical view of the nature of language than even many thinkers who are classified as linguistic analysts. His understanding of the complexity and flexibility of language places Ramsey squarely in the tradition of the later Wittgenstein. Moreover, there is a marked similarity between his view of language and that of such thinkers as J. L. Austin and Max Black.[29] The complexity of Ramsey's position also serves to distinguish him from some of the above thinkers who attempt to meet the empiricist challenge by interpreting religious languages as baldly empirical without qualification.

Perhaps the best way to sum up this preview of Ramsey's position is to call attention to the fact that the dominant theme of his writings is the insistence on a continuity which underlies all human discourse. All meaningful language, according to Ramsey, is both grounded in experience and logically odd in certain key respects. If this is true, then religious language is not uniquely problematic!

NOTES

1 A large part of this chapter appeared, prior to revisions, as 'The Meaning of Religious Language' in *Christianity Today*, IX, no. 8 (15 January 1965), p. 16.
2 Anthony Flew and Alasdair MacIntyre (eds), *New Essays in Philosophical Theology*, pp. 99–103.
3 ibid., pp. 101–2.
4 R. B. Braithwaite, *An Empiricist View of the Nature of Religious Belief*, p. 32.
5 Paul Tillich, *Systematic Theology*, I, p. 238.
6 ibid., p. 239.
7 ibid., p. 239.
8 ibid., p. 241.
9 ibid., p. 240.
10 Sidney Hook, (ed.), *Religious Experience and Truth*, p. 315.
11 *Systematic Theology*, pp. 100–5.
12 Paul Tillich, *Dynamics of Faith*, pp. 96–7; and *Systematic Theology*, pp. 100–5.
13 John H. Randall, 'Symposium: Are Religious Dogmas Cognitive and Meaningful?', *Journal of Philosophy*, LI, no. 5 (4 March 1954), p. 159; and *The Role of Knowledge in Western Religion*.
14 Michael Foster, *Mystery and Philosophy*.
15 Michael Foster, 'Contemporary British Philosophy and Christian Belief', *The Christian Scholar*, XLIII, no. 3 (Fall 1960), p. 196.
16 Willem Zuurdeeg, *An Analytical Philosophy of Religion*.
17 Willem Zuurdeeg, 'Implications of Analytical Philosophy for Theology', *Journal of Bible and Religion*, XXIX, no. 3 (July 1961), pp. 204.

18 This brief account of Hordern's position is adapted from my review of his book, *Speaking of God*, entitled 'The Talk Circle' in *The Christian Scholar*, XLVII, no. 1 (January 1966).

19 William Hordern, *Speaking of God*, p. 98.

20 Flew and MacIntyre (eds), *New Essays*, p. 105.

21 John Hick, *Faith and Knowledge*; 'Theology and Verification', *Theology Today*, XVIII, no. 1 (April 1960); *Philosophy of Religion*.

22 *Faith and Knowledge*, p. 150.

23 John Hutchison, *Language and Faith*.

24 ibid., pp. 129ff.

25 Frederick Ferré, *Language, Logic and God*; and 'Mapping the Logic of Models in Science and Theology', *The Christian Scholar*, XLVI, no. 1 (Spring 1963), pp. 9ff.

26 *Language, Logic and God*, p. 164.

27 ibid., p. 165.

28 Ian Ramsey, *Religious Language*.

29 Cf. especially the latter part of Austin's *How To Do Things With Words*; and Black's analysis of metaphor in his *Models and Metaphors*.

Part Two

RAMSEY'S POSITION:
A WIDER EMPIRICISM

Chapter 3

THE STRUCTURE OF RELIGIOUS EXPERIENCE

The whole of Bishop Ramsey's effort in the area of philosophical theology is directed by a twofold purpose. He is essentially interested in developing an account of religion which will preserve and enhance its concern with mystery, while maintaining and elucidating its basis in concrete human experience. Moreover, he is striving to maintain each of these concerns in a properly balanced relationship to one another. 'Theological language will be relevant when the situations it talks of match those of the world around us, and when links can then be traced between itself and the language we use to talk about the world.'[1]

Ramsey's concern with religious mystery needs some clarification. He insists that the sort of mystery inherent to religion must not be confused with that sort which can be cleared up by the gathering together of facts and information which were previously inaccessible. Nor should it be confused with the sort of mystery which is logically, and therefore permanently, inaccessible, since such mystery cannot be thought or talked about. Ramsey laments the fact that many religious thinkers, both past and present, have spoken about religious mystery in ways which imply these two confusions. The former approach to religion assumes that religious language is to be taken literally, and thus it not only invites serious philosophical difficulties, it fails to do justice to the complexity of religious discourse as well. With regard to the latter approach, however, Ramsey is equally insistent that religious mystery must not be reduced to the sort which bears no relationship at all to the facts of experience. In his view, a strictly symbolic view of religious language is as foreign to the concerns of Christian writers and worshippers as is a strictly literal view. The problem is to give an account of religious mystery in which it is possible for 'mystery and understanding to meet'. 'That which each of us knows, when he most significantly comes to himself in this way, is nothing at which we can satisfactorily point, it is nothing which can be "indicated demonstratively".'[2]

This reference to 'a wider empiricism' brings up the need for clarification of the second aspect of Ramsey's twofold concern, mentioned above. Here Ramsey directs his remarks in two directions: towards the theologian and towards the philosopher. To the former he maintains that, unless religious and theological language can be grounded in human experience, it ultimately will be both valueless and meaningless.

'. . . theological assertions must have a logical context which extends to, and is continuous with, those assertions of ordinary language for which sense experience is directly relevant. From such straightforward assertions, theological assertions must not be logically segregated: for that would mean that they were pointless and, in contrast to the only language which has an agreed meaning, meaningless.'[3]

At the same time, Ramsey maintains that the philosopher will have to broaden his conception of what counts as 'empirical'. Not only is such a broadening necessary to make it possible for religious discourse to have an empirical basis, it is necessary to do full justice to the actual facts concerning the complexity of human experience and language. To support this point Ramsey frequently calls upon the work of such contemporary philosophers as Wittgenstein, G. E. Moore, Gilbert Ryle, and J. L. Austin.

'. . . Wittgenstein would not allow other areas of discourse to be dismissed as "meaningless"—language was rich in its logical variety, and a major task of philosophy was to display and preserve this variety against all who held that evidence and criteria, if they be not scientific evidence and criteria, are worthless; and against all reductionists who would argue that "x is *nothing but* y," that "x is *really only* y".'[4]

Thus, it is to the most recent developments in empiricist philosophy that Ramsey turns for guidance and insight in his twofold task. He sees in mature empiricism, or linguistic analysis, both the tolerant spirit and the analytic methodology necessary for the construction of a balanced, reasonable, and theologically adequate account of the meaning of religious language. It is in this sense that

50

Ramsey can be said to accept the basic thrust of the challenge set forth by logical empiricism. He is impressed with the concern for meaning and verification expressed by this movement, and with its desire to develop reliable, if flexible, criteria with regard to the various uses of language. Moreover, he is convinced that the language philosophers, following the later Wittgenstein, are much more tolerant and sensitive toward language than were their positivistic forerunners. Ramsey believes 'that contemporary empiricism may revitalise our faith and our doctrine and make what seem so often to be the dry bones of theological discourse live'.[5]

One more introductory note needs to be sounded before more detailed examination of Ramsey's view can be given. Although he never explicitly states that this is the case, I am of the opinion that a particular view of the nature of religious experience provides an implicit foundation for Ramsey's entire approach. Put bluntly, my point is that Ramsey views religious experience as mediated through the other dimensions of experience, and not as immediate on the one hand, nor as impossible on the other hand. In other words, as will become extremely clear from his own discussion of what he terms 'religious disclosure', Ramsey maintains that religious experience is dependent upon other dimensions of experience, such as the sensory and the moral, but is not reducible to these other dimensions. Here he stands in the tradition of such thinkers as H. H. Farmer, John Oman, and most recently, John Hick,[6] in rejecting the view that religious experience is somehow *sui generis*.

Put into a linguistic framework, the same point can be made by saying that Ramsey seeks to follow a 'middle way' between interpreting talk about God as univocal and interpreting it as equivocal. Such terminology is used advisedly in order to draw attention to the similarity between Ramsey's view and that of Thomas Aquinas.[7] Little, if any, distortion results from roughly classifying Ramsey's position within the tradition which maintains the analogical nature of talk about God. There are, to be sure, differences, as well as similarities, between this tradition and Ramsey's approach.

Each of the foregoing considerations has been introduced in order to point out some of the dominant characteristics which underlie Ramsey's overall position concerning religious experience. It is time to move ahead to a more detailed examination of this position.

1 DISCLOSURE AND COMMITMENT

Ramsey, borrowing from Joseph Butler,[8] understands religious experience as exhibiting two salient characteristics. First, there is an awareness of a dimension of special significance arising out of ordinary experience. The essential claim of religion is that there is a depth to human experience which cannot be accounted for solely in terms of sensory description. 'Such a discernment lies at the basis of religion, whose characteristic claim is that there are situations which are spatio-temporal and more.'[9] Ramsey sees this awareness, or discernment, as the subjective aspect of what he calls a 'disclosure'. Second, there is in religious experience a response of total commitment to that which is discerned or disclosed in the depth-dimension of ordinary experience. This commitment, like its corresponding discernment, both arises from and goes beyond ordinary sensory experience.[10]

The examples which Ramsey gives of this type of 'disclosure-commitment' situation are many and varied. They can, however, be brought together under a hierarchical schema which provides in clarity and organisation more than it detracts by way of over-simplification. Without implying rigid lines of demarcation, Ramsey's examples of disclosure-commitment situations can be classified under the following headings: linguistic, perceptual, theoretic, moral, personal, and cosmic. I will discuss some of the specific examples which are found in Ramsey's various writings according to this classification, dealing first with the element of disclosure and concluding with some general remarks about commitment.

Once, in a small group discussion, Ramsey called attention to the following linguistic phenomena, both of which involve discernment.[11] The business of coming to grasp the meaning of words (as opposed to simply recognising letters) and of understanding sentences (as opposed to simply grasping words) clearly involves some sort of disclosure experience. Although the commonness of using language often causes adults to overlook its inscrutable character, anyone who has closely observed how children learn to speak and read their native tongue, or who has been engaged in learning a foreign language, can testify to the mystery involved in language. In like fashion, Ramsey maintained that the unending debate between universalists and nominalists is largely an attempt to come to grips with the disclosure involved in the use of class-terms. Without professing to solve the question, Ramsey briefly indicated that both parties are led astray by insisting that the main function of language is to name entities. He definitely wanted to maintain that understanding class-terms involves a disclosure which is based in, but which goes beyond, the naming of any entities whatsoever.

In his *Religious Language*, Ramsey develops examples of disclosures which take place within perceptual, especially visual, experience. Here he draws heavily upon the work of Gestalt psychology.

'Let us recall how there could be drawn twelve straight lines which at first sight might look no more than two squares with corners joined. But then there dawns on us "depth", and we see the twelve straight lines as a "unity". The lines indeed represent a cube and this cube may, as is well known, seem to enter into or stand out of the surface on which the lines are drawn. Here again is a characteristically different situation which dawns on us at some recognisable point. This is the point where twelve straight lines cease to be merely twelve straight lines, when a characteristically-different situation is evoked which needs odd words like "depth" and "unity", or mathematically the idea of a "new dimension", "volume" besides "area".'[12]

In other contexts, Ramsey mentions the recognition of an old friend, the rearrangement of pieces in a puzzle, and the way in which a series of polygons of an increasing number of sides may suggest a circle, as examples of perceptual situations that give rise to a disclosure which involves a dimension other than the sum of the particulars. This sort of example reminds one of Wittgenstein's discussion of seeing a particular picture 'as' a duck or 'as' a rabbit.[13]

The realms of mathematics and science are seen by Ramsey as involving disclosures which might be termed theoretic in nature. The way in which the axioms of Euclidean geometry, for instance, are 'seen' as 'self-evident' by the beginning student suggests a conceptual understanding that goes beyond simply understanding the meaning of the sentence involved.[14] Although Ramsey does not mention them, it seems that one could offer the grasping of the rules for deductive and inductive inference as further examples of theoretic situations in which a special discernment is implied. One other example which Ramsey borrows from mathematics pertains to the way in which the concept of 'infinite' is delineated in the use of such phrases as 'infinite sum'.[15] Although it bears certain similarities to other sums, it can never be fully explained in terms of them. From observing its use in actual situations one 'discerns' what it means. Perhaps the same could be said for the symbol zero'.

Elsewhere, Ramsey goes to some length to establish the fact that in the construction of scientific hypotheses and laws, the scientist makes use of disclosures which go beyond the data at hand.[16] In the former instance, the scientist often conceives a causal pattern among various phenomena on the basis of an extremely small amount of data. Moreover, even when the hypothesis thus conceived has been confirmed by a vast amount of data, the resultant 'law' is still only a highly refined generalisation which needs to be qualified by talk about 'normal conditions' and 'experimental error'. Ramsey wants to maintain that in making such a generalisation, the scientist is giving expression to a discernment which is based in, and yet goes beyond, the actual facts. This same sort of analysis would seem to shed some light upon the contemporary debate concerning the justification of induction, if such justification were seen as the justification of an insight.

Moving on to examples of disclosure which are humanistically more significant, it is important to give attention to what may be called moral discernment. Ramsey uses such examples because he is convinced that the disclosures which are the most significant religiously are those which centre in personal and inter-personal relationships. Although he discusses moral discernment in *Religious Language*,[17] the most illuminating accounts of it are found in Ramsey's frequent articles, and for this reason the following discussion will focus on them.

In a review of a lecture on 'Reason and Experience in Ethics',[18] Ramsey takes a definite stand against the tendency in contemporary ethical theory to segregate ethical discourse off from other uses of language as *sui generis*. He maintains that moral judgements must be based in, and thus are closely related to, the judgements of psychology and sociology. It is impossible for ethical discourse to take place in a vacuum. Nevertheless, ethical judgements cannot be reduced to factual judgements. This dilemma, which forms the very heart of contemporary ethical debate, can only be overcome, according to Ramsey, by acknowledging the fact that ethical judgements result from disclosures which go beyond, but are not independent of, the factual elements of a given situation. When a duty is discerned, or an ethical judgement is made, a disclosure has been mediated by the spatio-temporal facts; a disclosure which, although common in everyday experience, is not exhaustible in terms of straightforward, descriptive language.

Ramsey gives a concrete example of this type of ethical disclosure in his essay 'On the Possibility and Purpose of a Metaphysical Theology'.[19] With respect to the situation in which a man sweeping up the litter on Hampstead Heath comes across a letter written by his son or daughter, Ramsey states that the moral question of whether or not the man should read the letter can only be decided by a consideration of all the facts of the situation.

'We recognise something as an obligation and duty, when . . . it presents itself to us within a disclosure situation. But it is notorious that there can be "conflicts" of duty—the Hampstead Heath sweeper may think he has a duty to exert a protective providence over his son or his daughter; equally well a duty to respect his or her privacy. We then have the prospect of a disclosure presenting us with two challenges which generate conflicting responses. The only way to resolve the difficulty is to develop the empirical details in each case until there arises within the one disclosure a single challenge and response.'[20]

Another example of moral discernment is mentioned by Ramsey in connection with his discussion of Joseph Butler.[21] The sense of moral obligation which a bystander experiences when a child is drowning gives evidence of a disclosure. A purely physical description of the situation does not exhaust the sense of duty. In fact, it would always be possible to say, 'Well, there goes another blob of protoplasm'. Nevertheless, it is just as true that the sense of duty does not occur apart from a cognition of the facts.

In like manner, our knowledge of other persons, *qua* persons, involves a disclosure which arises out of, but cannot be equated with, our knowledge and talk of their behaviour. Since this aspect of experience is integral to morality, it is appropriate to discuss it at this juncture. Ramsey often uses examples of how we come to know other persons—and become aware that they are more than the sum total of their physical behaviour—by the introduction of one additional fact which serves to integrate and give depth to all the other facts we know about the person.[22] There are striking, and unaccidental, parallels between what Ramsey has to say on this subject and what philosophers like Gilbert Ryle and P. F. Strawson have to say about the problem of knowing other minds.[23] In each case there is an emphasis on the fact that our knowledge of other persons 'goes beyond' our knowledge of their behaviour, not in the sense that an inductive hypothesis goes beyond the data, but in the sense that we begin and do not conclude, by speaking and behaving towards others as persons. In Strawson's terminology, this is one of the senses in which the concept of person can be said to be 'logically primitive'.[24]

Perhaps the most illuminating illustration which Ramsey gives of the type of disclosure involved in the knowledge of other persons is the one concerning the conversation between Robin Hood and the Tinker who was out to arrest him.

'The Tinker unexpectedly meets Robin Hood and the conversation proceeds like this:

Q. Do you know Robin Hood?
A. Oh, very well indeed, I have the closest knowledge of him.
Q. Where is he now, I wonder?
A. I am sure he cannot be very far away.
Q. Is he strong?
A. Fairly so. He had a successful bout with a very skilled wrestler the other day.
Q. How tall is he?
A. Just about my height.
Q. Colour of hair?
A. Brown.
Q. Is he clever?
A. He has misled a lot of folk.

Now supposing Robin Hood had concluded such question-and-answering like this: "And I'm the man". What would be added by this claim that "It is I"? There are two possible answers. Some might say, as I have admitted, that "I" is purely indicative. It just says: What you see now, this body, this chap talking with you, is of a part with all we have been describing. Nor can this be denied. The leading question is: Is that all? For another answer is possible. When Robin makes his confession, there might be a disclosure. The sequence to date, plus the pattern before the Tinker, then becomes part of a disclosure situation where the Tinker discerns around "Robin Hood" an objective challenge.'[25]

Here again one can see the basic disclosure-pattern involved in personal knowledge. Clearly, the facts which are freely given by Robin while incognito are of real importance for a knowledge of Robin Hood. None the less, they are given a new 'depth' when experientially related to the one additional statement, 'It is I!' In Ramsey's oft-used phrase, 'the light dawns, the penny drops', and a whole new perspective is revealed. This type of situation takes place quite frequently within the framework of intimate friendships as well. Our knowledge of close friends and loved ones is related to, but is more than the sum of our observations of their behaviour. In fact, it is often the case that our knowledge of them as persons makes it possible for us to observe and understand certain aspects of their behaviour more adequately. In Ramsey's words:

> 'When such a disclosure occurs around a human pattern we speak of knowing people as they "really are", of there being "deep" affection between us, of loving them "for themselves". . . . "Husband", "mother", "father", "friend"—these are words which while they are undoubtedly associated with certain characteristic behaviour patterns have a transcendent reference as well—and are grounded in disclosures.'[26]

The foregoing discussion of the disclosure-nature of knowledge of other persons provides a transitional step between moral discernments and discernments of personal identity. Although he does not opt for an identification of the two, Ramsey does think that often the clearest way to call attention to the nature of religious experience is by exploring the nature of self-knowledge. Even though our knowledge of ourselves is in some respects similar to our knowledge of others, there are certain unique factors as well. An understanding of Ramsey's analysis of self-knowledge is essential to an understanding of his concept of religious experience.

Ramsey's analysis of self-knowledge has both an experiential and a linguistic side. I will deal only with the former at this time, leaving the latter until the next chapter. Ramsey's thesis with regard to our own knowledge of ourselves as persons is, (1) that we obviously do know ourselves as persons, and (2) that such knowledge cannot be equated with a knowledge of our behaviour. Moreover, as will be seen more fully in the next chapter, no description of our behaviour can ever exhaust our self-knowledge for the simple reason that the logic of first-person statements is distinct from that of third-person statements. 'Here then is a "fact"—my own existence as I know it, in its full subjectivity—which eludes, and in principle, any exhaustive direct description.'[27]

This knowledge of ourselves is, according to Ramsey, the result of a disclosure which breaks in on us in relationship to our day-by-day empirical experience. Although no one ever has what would be called straightforward empirical experience of himself as a self, every person does, in so far as he is a person at all, come to use the term 'I', and to tacitly develop a concept of the self.[28] This self-awareness arises out of our experience of objects and behaviour, but it cannot be reduced experientially nor logically, to such experience. In a word, 'it is disclosed to us, it breaks in on us at some point or other as the descriptive story is ever more fully built up".[29]

Although he maintains that 'That which each of us knows, when he most significantly comes to himself in this way, is nothing at which we can satisfactorily point, it is nothing which can be "indicated demonstratively",'[30] Ramsey endeavours to 'tell stories' and give examples of situations in which such self-awareness can be seen to be active. He calls attention to party games which have as their object the identification of some person, on the basis of certain clues. In no case is any one clue logically sufficient, but often one clue, or a pattern of several, will give rise to a disclosure.[31] In like fashion, he considers the problem of personal identity as only being a problem for people other than the person in question.[32] No matter how similar in appearance and factual data they are, both the impostor and the genuine person know which is which. Presumably, this even obtains in the case of amnesia, in the sense that at any given moment the person involved knows that he is who he is—in Ryle's words 'a tautology worth remembering'.

In connection with the story of Nathan's parabolic accusation of David, Ramsey summarises the main aspects of his view of disclosure:

'But if there is "more", where the "more" cannot be perceptually verified, we return to our question . . . what is its empirical basis? How do we come to recognise this "more"? The answer is: In a disclosure, a disclosure in which I come to myself and realise myself as more than the observable behaviour I display. The stock example of such a disclosure is that of David and Nathan, when at Nathan's "Thou art the man!" David comes to himself, the "penny drops" and the disclosure occurs. What "I" distinctively stands for, what I am to myself more than I as he is to you, is something which *a fortiori cannot be described*. It can only be evoked in and for each of us, and that means given (as we have said) in a disclosure that justifies our use of "I" in the extended sense, the sense which belongs to a situation not restricted to the observables in terms of which other people (as well as I) can talk of it.'[33]

Although he enjoins the use of caution in this connection, Ramsey acknowledges the close relationship which exists between such self-knowledge and the sort of thing existentialist writers have in mind when they speak of 'participation', 'involvement', 'authentic existence', and the like.[34] 'In this way . . . I can agree with those who, following Kierkegaard and other existentialists, stress the significance of what is called "the realisation of one's existence as a self", or "choosing oneself". . . .'[35]

Having laid the groundwork for understanding Ramsey's concept of disclosure by means of the foregoing examples, it is time to move to a consideration of the concept of religious disclosure proper. Ramsey often uses the term 'cosmic disclosure' in his discussion of this type of experience. It is absolutely essential to be perfectly clear at the outset about the one most important characteristic of religious, or cosmic, disclosure. Even as the disclosures discussed above are always mediated through empirical situations, religious disclosures are always so mediated as well. Moreover, and this is equally as important, Ramsey views religious disclosures as mediated through the above-mentioned disclosures themselves! That is to say, disclosures of what may be called 'the divine dimension' do not occur in an experiential vacuum, but rather arise out of perceptual, conceptual, moral, and personal disclosures, which in turn arise out of empirical settings.

In the small group discussion referred to earlier, Ramsey made the above point quite emphatically that cosmic disclosures, which give rise to talk about God and His activity, are mediated by means of more common disclosures. He defined a cosmic disclosure in terms of discerning something about total reality through the disclosures of everyday life. They are special cases of the genus 'disclosure' which can happen, but need not happen, at any level of experience. Thus, religious people speak of moral duty as 'God's will', and of 'seeing God in their friends'. Ramsey even suggests from time to time that the classical proofs of God's existence arose because of the cosmic disclosures which people experienced in connection with such concepts as 'being', 'cause', 'perfection', and the like.[36] In this particular group discussion Ramsey even suggested that the term 'God' might be viewed as a class term for all cosmic disclosures, and as such it would bear similarities—as well as marked differences—to a proper name.

Although he nowhere states the important point concerning the mediated relationship between religious and non-religious disclosure as explicitly as he did in the above-mentioned discussion, Ramsey clearly implies it in several of his writings. I quote the following statements as representative of this implied emphasis:

'. . . my next suggestion is that the human case acts as a catalyst for the cosmic case, and it is as and when a cosmic disclosure is thereby evoked that we are able to speak of God—what the cosmic disclosure discloses—in terms of the models with which the finite situations have supplied us.'[37]

and elsewhere: '. . . in every disclosure the object can eventually bear the name "God" '.[38]

It is in this way, then, that Ramsey understands what has been traditionally classified as religious experience. When one speaks of experiencing God he is calling attention to a discernment in which there has been disclosed to him a cosmic dimension of reality by means of the more common disclosures arising out of experiential situations. A person's awareness of God is similar to his awareness of objects (as opposed to 'sense data'), moral obligation, and persons (including himself). All of this, of course, is not to say that the claimed awareness of God is as common as these other aware-nesses, nor that it is necessarily a veridical experience. The questions concerning the confirmation of disclosures will have to be dealt with in Chapter Five. What has been discussed up to this point is the 'empirical-fact-and-more' nature of natural and religious disclosure. According to Ramsey, religious experience is seen to be continuous with certain important aspects of everyday experience, when the latter are understood in terms of their disclosure nature.

One more very important aspect of Ramsey's interpretation of religious experience remains to be discussed. In every disclosure situation, on whatever level of experience, there is an element of what Ramsey terms 'commitment'. That is to say, whenever a dis-closure 'dawns' it gives rise to a corresponding commitment to act in a way which is appropriate to that which is being disclosed. In fact, it is possible to say that such commitment is what distinguishes a disclosure-situation from one which is routine or 'flat'. Thus it is through people's actions that their commitments are known, and through their commitments that their disclosures are known.

The universality of this element of commitment in all disclosure-situations can be seen by re-examining briefly the examples of dis-closure discussed in the first part of this section. The grasping and using of words, sentences, and class-terms obviously involve a commitment in the sense that one's entire linguistic behaviour is based upon the disclosure of this type of meaning. In this case, as in those which are to follow, it is important to avoid thinking of commitment exclusively in terms of an explicit, conscious response. As often as not, the commitments accompanying disclosures are tacit, but none the less real. The perception of objects and patterns also involves a tacit commitment which is appropriate to what is disclosed, as is evidenced by our ability to navigate among pieces of furniture and to master highly difficult skills.

As one moves up the scale of increasingly complex disclosures, the corresponding commitments become more and more explicit and conscious. Grasping concepts like 'axiom', 'infinite', 'causation', and 'probability' involves a commitment to a certain procedure in the disciplines of mathematics and science. Seeing the point of moral discourse and relating to others as persons involves disclosures which express clear-cut commitments to that which is disclosed therein, namely duty and personality. In the same way, our personal knowledge of ourselves results in a commitment, however implicit, concerning our own free activity and first person discourse. Both of these commitments will be discussed in more detail later on. The overall point being made at this juncture is that on whatever level of human experience they occur, disclosures give rise to attitudinal and behavioural commitments which are commensurate with that which is disclosed therein.

The cosmic discernment which bears religious significance also evokes a commitment appropriate to its object. Although religious commitment is similar in certain respects to that of other forms of discernment, it has its own unique characteristics as well. At the very least it is more comprehensive and carries more depth than any other commitments. Ramsey puts it this way:

'So far we have seen two kinds of discernment-commitment—"mathematical" commitment and "personal" or "quasi-personal" commitment. Religious commitment, I suggest, partakes of both. It combines the total commitment to a pastime, to a ship, to a person, with the breadth of mathematical commitment. It combines the "depth" of personal or quasi-personal loyalty—to a sport, a boat, a loved one—with the range of mathematical and scientific devotion. It is a commitment suited to the whole job of living—not one just suited to building houses, or studying inter-planetary motion, or even one suited to our own families, and no more.'[39]

It is common knowledge that religious experience often brings about this high sense of commitment which, when properly interpreted, sheds light upon the totality of a person's heretofore non-religious commitments and experiences. What is not common knowledge, and what Ramsey is concerned to point out, is that the experiential logic of religious commitment is essentially similar to that of commitments involved at other levels of experience. Such an emphasis helps in the understanding of both religious commitment and non-religious commitment. The religious person's talk about God is to be understood as arising out of a disclosure-commitment situation which, in turn, both results from, and sheds light upon, the rest of his experience. Such talk will be related to object-language and will go beyond it as well.

> 'So our conclusion is that for the religious man "God" is a key word, an irreducible posit, an ultimate of explanation expressive of the kind of *commitment* he professes. It is to be talked about in terms of the object-language over which it presides, but only when this object-language is qualified; in which case this qualified object-language becomes also currency for that odd *discernment* with which religious *commitment*, when it is not bigotry or fanaticism, will necessarily be associated.'[40]

This then is the pattern of religious experience according to Ramsey's interpretation. It remains to be said that he associates revelation with cosmic disclosure. Perhaps it will be helpful to view this type of disclosure under the heading of 'general' revelation, and the type of disclosure peculiar to Christianity under the heading of 'special' or 'historic' revelation. Some additional aspects of cosmic disclosure, namely those of freedom and immortality, will be discussed in the next section. Some of the intricacies of historic disclosure will be taken up in the final section of this chapter, entitled 'Miracles'. It should be noted that this approach to revelation stands midway between those which view it as strictly informational on the one hand, and those which view it as strictly existential on the other hand. The same relationship obtains with regard to the more extreme views of religious experience. Ramsey is holding out for a view which will do justice to both the mystery and the empirical nature of religious experience.

2 FREEDOM AND IMMORTALITY

In addition to disclosure-commitment situations which are of special religious significance because they give rise to talk of 'experiencing

God', there are, according to Ramsey, other disclosure-commitment situations which have religious significance as well. Many of these cluster around experiences involving decision and action, while others focus on questions concerning life and death. Such disclosure-situations give rise to talk about 'freedom' and 'immortality', respectively. Although Ramsey's account of these experiences and concepts is quite extensive, especially with reference to their linguistic implications, in this section I shall mainly consider their ramifications for the explication of Ramsey's view of religious experience.

The main drive of Ramsey's discussion of freedom and immortality is, as one would expect, in close harmony with the position delineated in the first section of this chapter. He is primarily concerned to call attention to the fact that there are aspects of our decision-action experiences, and of our life-death experiences, which, although they arise out of, and are dependent upon, empirical and factual considerations, transcend the empirical dimension of experience. In spite of the fact that such aspects of these experiences cannot be captured in descriptive language, they are known to be the case by many, if not most, people. Moreover, an awareness, or discernment, of these aspects can be evoked by attending to the subtleties of the language employed with respect to such situations. Such discernment is, in fact, often the primary purpose of such language.

Before proceeding with an analysis of Ramsey's discussion of freedom and immortality, an important caveat, which applies to the considerations of the first section of this chapter as well as to the present section, needs to be inserted. In this context Ramsey's comments about disclosure-commitment situations, focusing on God, freedom, and immortality, are not to be construed as arguments for the verification of the claim that the referents of these concepts actually exist. Ramsey is primarily concerned with exploring the logic of such situations and locutions in order to establish their meaningfulness. That is to say, he simply wants to maintain that such claims are not as 'far out' and logically preposterous as is often maintained. The question of the truth of such claims is another matter, and will be taken up in Chapter Five. In this chapter I am only concerned with Ramsey's claim that religious discourse involving terms like 'God', 'freedom', and 'immortality' is justified as significant by its anchor in human experience and ordinary language.

Ramsey's analysis of the language and experiences related to the concept of freedom is very closely related to his analysis of self-knowledge as set forth in section one. He begins by outlining the opposing positions of the historic debate concerning determinism and freewill.[41] Determinism's essential claim is that human behaviour is, in principle, describable and predictable exclusively in terms of spatio-temporal language. 'Critical' indeterminism, on the other hand, claims that some (fortunately, not all) human behaviour, most notably that involving decisions and actions, eludes, in principle, such description and prediction. Ramsey takes moral decisions and actions as the most obvious example of human behaviour which is not reducible to object-language.

The primary argument offered by Ramsey in favour of the freewill position is an appeal to the facets of ordinary language which are portrayed in talk about decisions and actions. Such language not only has freedom of decision built into it, but it defies all attempts to eliminate it without eliminating the vast majority of ordinary language at the same time. On the basis of the actual examples of free choice which Ramsey gives to substantiate his claim, it is safe to conclude that he assumes, and I think rightly, that such a price is too inflationary to accept. This is clearly an example of an appeal to what J. L. Austin termed 'linguistic phenomenology'. The underlying conviction of such an appeal is that ordinary language contains most of the important distinctions that need to be made concerning experienceable reality.[42] Ramsey summarises his position in the following words:

'So the claim of free will is the claim that at a moment of "free" decision there occurs a situation not restricted to the spatio-temporal events it contains—those events which are the "objects" in terms of which everyone, including me, will describe it afterwards. We have argued that this claim can be justified by reflecting on such ordinary language as (*pace* some contemporary philosophers) does justice to the complexity of ordinary situations. We make a "free" decision when we are not just this or that behaviour pattern, but when we are "men", when each of us is distinctively "I". At such moments of decision, when all of us characteristically use of ourselves the word "I", this word covers more than all language about objects or all scientific language talks about. . . . We can all readily recognise the point of a psychologist's mythology. But all that granted, the believer in free will holds that in a certain kind of decision action a man realises himself as something more than language or all of these stories—be they of biochemistry, economics, psychology, and so on—talk about.'[43]

Next, Ramsey embarks upon a detailed examination of the logical and experiential relations between free decisions and moral responsibility. Just as our inability to capture our decision-making activity within the limitations of object-language gives rise to a subjective disclosure of self-hood and freedom, so our awareness of our self-hood and freedom gives rise to an objective disclosure of moral responsibility which 'transcends the observables through which it is expressed'.[44] To put it another way, even as our knowledge of our own person and free choice are mediated through the subtleties of our decisions and actions, so our awareness of moral obligation is mediated through the juxtaposition of freedom of choice and the spatio-temporal factors of our relationship to other persons. It simply is impossible to reduce the experience and talk of moral duty to talk of causal determinism.[45] It is, incidentally, this transcendent character of moral obligation which Ramsey believes has led philosophers such as Kant to talk about 'Absolute Duty', and the like.[46]

Ramsey provides many illuminating examples, which cannot be examined in detail, by way of evoking a 'disclosure' of the nature of moral disclosure in the mind of the reader. After discussing the way in which the Good Samaritan's response exemplifies how moral obligation arises from, but goes beyond, empirical details and routine behaviour patterns,[47] Ramsey examines the situation of a terrified child aboard a sinking ship by way of pointing up these same factors. He concludes:

'Then a steward catches sight of a small child crying for his parents. In one way, here is just another noise on a ship full of men and women shouting and brawling and behaving like terror-stricken animals. But for the steward it is otherwise. He at once "sees" his Duty. Here is an additional empirical feature—the cry of the child—which transforms the whole situation. At once the steward becomes a man again. He sits with the child, cares for him and comforts him. Eventually, both are drowned together, but without panic or struggle. A catalogue of the spatio-temporal features would not in the end be vastly different than it would have been whatever the steward had done. But the last ten minutes on the ship exemplified a challenge and a response which was characteristically dutiful, for both challenge and response transcended the empirical situation through which they were expressed.'[48]

Finally, Ramsey is concerned to show the logical and experiential relationship between disclosures and talk about moral duty on the one hand, and disclosures and talk about God on the other. In so doing he hopes to show the religious significance of decisive and moral experience, and to thereby establish the significant possibility (but not the validity) of religious experience and language.

Ramsey develops his argument in the context of the discussion between Bertrand Russell and A. J. Ayer over the relation of God-talk to absolute duty-talk.[49] Although Russell, unlike Ayer, admitted a belief in absolute values, both he and Ayer agreed that the existence or non-existence of God is totally irrelevant to the question of the existence of such values. Ayer, in fact, maintained that it is inconsistent to believe that values are both absolute and validated by divine authority. In the first place, Ramsey is concerned to point out that Russell's belief in absolute ethical values, in spite of his inability to demonstrate their existence, points up the possibility of moral disclosure. Ramsey argues that Russell's own statements, which focus on situations involving 'wanton cruelty' and the like, imply that his belief in absolute values derives from a discernment-commitment experience.[50] Second, Ramsey argues that although moral experience and discourse can operate logically independent of religious experience and discourse, it is also true that the two realms can be meshed in a complementary fashion. The main point here is that God-talk is capable of including·duty-talk, but cannot be exhausted by it.

'The basic justification for the word "God", then, is that in talking about the universe, in reckoning with distinctive situations, we find that we need to talk of more than Duty and Absolute Value. "God" thus takes its place with the various words and phrases which one by one specify what is distinctively objective about this or that disclosure-situation.'[51]

To put it differently, talk about God maps a larger area than, but also includes, talk about duty and morality. In this sense it can be said to function, and to thus prove its value, as an 'integrating' term, or concept. Although such statements as 'X is my duty' and 'X is God's will' are 'alternative and complementary assertions viewing the same situation through two different language frames',[52]

66

Ramsey maintains that the latter is not superfluous, since it serves the function of integrating the talk of duty with a variety of other experiences and locutions.

> 'Our conclusion is that . . . we may nevertheless say, in addition to saying that "I ought to do X" and "X is my duty", that "X is God's will for me". In saying this we are in fact using such a phrase as "God's will" to give us an alternative description for what confronts us when we are aware of obligation, an alternative description which seeks to do justice to the fact that there are distinctive disclosure-situations other than those in which "Duty" is pegged. So the one key word "God" includes, and has a wider use than, the other key word "Duty".[53]

In a more recent writing,[54] Ramsey maintains that moral discourse arises out of a discernment of an objective 'claim' which discloses itself in and by the moral situation. He thinks that the acknowledgement of this claim-making disclosure is what is lacking from the views of many contemporary moral philosophers. Without this disclosure the prescriptive and universal force of ethical statements has no foundation. Moreover, Ramsey indicates that in addition to its integrating function with respect to the language of morals in relation to other regions of language, theological language can serve to call attention to this claim-making disclosure. In this way God-talk can be used to 'enrich' talk about duty and correct conduct without jeopardising the latter's autonomy.

Ramsey concludes his discussion of freedom by suggesting that such a view of the relation between moral experience and religious experience has the additional value of disposing of such age-old riddles as whether an action is right because it is God's will, or whether it is God's will because it is right; and secondly whether God's omnipotence negates individual freedom. Such 'pseudo-problems' only arise when we confuse the moral and the religious language-games, or when we suppose that talk of God's power, i.e. 'omnipotence', follows talk about physical power in an unqualified manner. If we keep the language functions separate and base our God-talk in situations which are distinctively personal, we can, according to Ramsey, avoid many of the pitfalls traditionally associated with religious experience and language.[55]

Like Kant, but for somewhat different reasons, Ramsey thinks that the question of immortality is closely linked to the question of freedom. Whereas Kant argued from the reality of duty and freedom to the reality of immortality, Ramsey is content to indicate how an awareness of duty and freedom can give rise to a disclosure of what immortality might mean. Since a sensitivity to the various aspects of decision-making discloses a self which transcends, in not being reducible to, the dimension of spatio-temporal experience, it is not difficult, in Ramsey's view, to conceive of how this self could transcend physical death.[56]

Ramsey begins by setting out 'to show that typical arguments against immortality derive their point from stressing our public "impersonal" behaviour, and from restricting and belittling our "personal" significance',[57] and that, contrariwise, arguments in favour of immortality stress the latter in addition to acknowledging the former. As usual, the main force of his procedure is to present and examine situations which are distinctively personal in order to enable the reader to discern the significance of language about immortality. Such procedure is, to borrow a phrase from Kierkegaard, a means of 'indirect communication'. Ramsey thinks it is justified by the systematically elusive nature of personal knowledge with respect to the 'direct communication' of object-language.

Examples are taken from morality and psychical research, as well as from world religions and the renewing processes of nature. The disclosure-commitment situation focusing on duty is likened to that focusing on truth. In both cases there is a concern for the empirical facts of the situation, plus a discernment of, and commitment to, something more than these facts as well. This additional factor is not a concern for some metaphysical abstraction, but neither can it be exhausted by speaking of a 'subjective drive', or what have you. Such disclosures are said to disclose a transcendent dimension which, since it can never be exhausted by a description, or increase, of empirical factors, might well be talked about in terms of immortality.

> 'In this way never-ending stories about searching after truth become an appropriate technique for evoking a situation which, when it breaks in on us, we shall then call "*the* Truth", and see its challenge as one of Duty. And when that happens, we likewise know ourselves as transcending the spatio-temporal, never exhaustively described by object stories. We are assured of our immortality.'[58]

After granting the difficulties involved, Ramsey suggests that the phenomena of psychical research serve both (1) to recreate a sense of wonder and mystery in a world from which such elements are far too often systematically eliminated, and (2) to indicate 'that there is an element in personal intercourse beyond the observable behaviour with which we normally associate it'.[59] Although it clearly proves nothing, in the strict sense of 'prove', Ramsey maintains that the temporal and geographical universality of a belief in immortality is worthy of more than the short shrift it often receives.[60] The common analogies which are drawn between immortality and the renewing processes of nature, such as winter turning into spring and sleep turning into waking, are of no value, according to Ramsey, as analogical arguments. Nevertheless, he thinks they do have value in evoking a disclosure of the kind of thing meant in language about immortality.[61] First-person talk about death, in fact, is seen to be logically odd when contrasted to first-person talk about sleep. The logical uniqueness of first-person utterances was discussed in the first section of this chapter, and will be dealt with more thoroughly at the outset of the next chapter.

Next, Ramsey moves to a discussion of some of the linguistic ramifications of such a view of the experiential basis of belief in immortality. Since these considerations are more appropriate to the concerns of the next chapter, I will postpone any discussion of them at this juncture. It should be noted, however, that Ramsey presents an analysis of the concept of the soul which dissolves many traditional philosophical and theological debates. He denies the platonic dualism often associated with Christian belief, and on the basis of an examination of several Old Testament texts, shows that the Hebrew term for soul often refers to the whole person. It is thus a synonym for 'I' or 'person', and not the name of a ghost which is imprisoned in a body.

'In short, my conclusion is that the philosopher can welcome the contemporary Christian emphasis on the Hebrew use of the word "soul", which is a much better guide to its logical behaviour than language which suggests that the soul is some kind of counterpart, but hidden, object. The Hebrews showed implicit logical good sense when . . . they used the "immortality of the soul" as a synonym for the "immortality of I".'[62]

Ramsey concludes by discussing the significance of talk about immortality which includes references to a 'future life'.[63] Since the major point of concern in this chapter is Ramsey's view of religious experience, I shall not enter into a consideration of the details of

69

this discussion. Much of what he says under this head is more concerned with religious language than with religious experience, and will be discussed in the next chapter. In addition, much of what he says is specifically theological in its concern, and is not central to the philosophical thrust of this present study. Suffice it to say that here again Ramsey emphasises that all talk about immortality and a future life, like all talk about persons, freedom, and duty, must be grounded in experiential situations which disclose this transcendent dimension. The sorts of situations which do this best are those which focus on purposive fulfilment, moral retribution, and personal love.[64]

In response to Anthony Flew's contention that, although 'I' is not reducible to bodily features, there can be no meaningful talk of an 'I' existing after death,[65] Ramsey maintains that such a conclusion only follows if one assumes that 'I' can be equated with observable behaviour. On the contrary, Ramsey suggests, '. . . there are certain characteristically personal situations . . . which are not wholly tractable in terms of (public) behaviour stories. . . .'[66] In addition to pointing out that the ambiguity of the term 'death' casts serious doubts on the validity of equating it with 'the end of all life', Ramsey offers funerals as examples of situations which can evoke an awareness that self-existence is more than observable behaviour. Once again, he appeals to the logical oddness of first-person statements as evidence that self-existence is known, even though it can never be fully stated nor argued for.

The foregoing analysis of Ramsey's discussion of freedom and immortality was undertaken in order to cast further light on his concept of disclosure-commitment situations which comprise his interpretation of religious experience. Nearly all of the aspects of Ramsey's thought which have been examined thus far pertain to religious experience in general. It is time to consider that aspect of his thought which relates to Christian experience more exclusively. It is his discussion of miracles that focuses on the revelatory nature of historical experience most clearly, and consequently the next section will be devoted to this theme.

3   MIRACLES AND THE RESURRECTION

In the following account of Ramsey's interpretation of the concept of miracle, I shall begin with the way in which he locates the concept in general, and then I shall move to the specific conclusions he draws from his general view concerning the miracles of Jesus. All the while, I shall attempt to focus his view in such a way as to shed light upon his interpretation of Christian experience in terms of disclosure-commitment situations.

Ramsey begins by examining 'the broad characteristics of the languages of natural science, of history, and of metaphysics' by way of asking 'whether a place can be found anywhere, and if so in what sort of setting, for the word "miracles" '.[67] Taking the language of science first, he examines some typical scientific assertions, such as 'water boils at 100° C.', and draws two conclusions. First, science begins with statements which express observations and low-level generalisations, the latter of which clearly go beyond what is given in direct observation. Second, science moves away from this more concrete level towards higher abstraction by constructing ever broader hypotheses. In this latter stage, the scientist tries to include as many facts as possible, while excluding those that do not conform to the uniformity which his hypothesis expresses. Thus scientific language is always seeking to expand by modifying, or converting itself as it goes.[68]

Going further, Ramsey maintains that scientific language has two permanent limitations. First, it is always incomplete, because the facts will always be inexhaustible and because it always seeks a higher level of generality than that which it has been able to realise. Second, scientific language is made possible and valuable precisely because it begins by selecting certain features (and thus ignoring others) and progresses by moving away from these features toward increasing abstraction. Thus it strives to transcend concrete particulars.

'In the face then of such inadequacies as we have just mentioned, scientific language could hardly claim of itself to offer total coverage in the sense of being a completely *adequate* account of all facts as they are *concretely* given. Scientific language may detail uniformities more and more comprehensively; but its very success in so doing means that its pictures are more and more outline sketches of concrete, given fact.'[69]

On the basis of these limitations, Ramsey concludes that scientific language stands in need of 'boundary words' which lie outside of the language-game of science, but which also serve both to unite the various languages of science and to provide the concrete, factual reference of their abstractions. Such words might be termed 'metaphysical words', as long as this term is not construed to be function-

71

ing in some 'superscientific' or descriptive fashion.[70] Only by the use of such terms can the built-in limitations of scientific language be transcended.

From all of this it is plain, according to Ramsey, that scientific language leaves no room for the word 'miracle'. Any and all irregularities must be either ignored or reduced to regularities by the language of science. This is the commitment that is built into the assumptions and goals of strictly scientific inquiry. But such a commitment cuts both ways, in Ramsey's view, and thus it is equally true that science cannot say that miracles do not occur. All that can be said is that within the language-game of science, no such concept is used, or needed.[71] The question of the use and need of such concepts outside of science, as 'boundary words', is entirely another question. An obvious corollary of this conclusion is that all the traditional debates about whether or not miracles 'break' the laws of nature have been a vast waste of time and energy. Not only is it inappropriate to speak of descriptive laws being 'broken', it can be clearly seen that in some sense science and religion are speaking two different, although not unrelated, language games. The activity of God is not a scientific hypothesis!

It is clear from the above argument that miracles are only discredited by being thus eliminated from scientific discourse if one assumes that such discourse is the only sort of meaningful language there is. In order to explore the possibility of finding another meaningful context for the concept of miracle, Ramsey moves to an examination of the language of history. Although there are, following the contemporary understanding of history, certain crucial differences between the languages of science and history, Ramsey is concerned to maintain that there are certain crucial similarities as well. Both the differences and the similarities are relevant to an understanding of miracle.

Unlike science, history is concerned to focus on and present concrete events and features in such a way as to preserve and elucidate them in relationship to their own and present-day situations. In a word, history seeks to be concrete, while science seeks to be abstract. This concreteness is expressed in terms of persons and events.

> '. . . historical language is a technique for naming and organising *at a concrete level of personal encounter*, such a selection of facts as endeavours to repeat certain "events as they occurred", and thus to bring them into relation with contemporary experience

. . . history is pre-eminently concerned with *persons*. Its distinctive feature is to use person-words as part of its technique for comprehensiveness, to use person-patterns in its search for concreteness. Its language portrays a pattern of personal events as a clue to the totality, "past", "present", and even "future", which it tries to interpret.'[72]

Like science, however, history also involves the use of selectivity and key terms which provide the context within which the language of history finds its meaning and significance. The concept 'person', even when objectified in terms of 'wage-earner', 'serf' or 'king', is seen by Ramsey to function as a boundary word, or an irreducible posit, in relation to the language of history. 'Only from another sort of language altogether does the language of history find its necessary means of selection and extension at a personal level.'[73]

Here, again, one can see the relevance of metaphysical language. It is Ramsey's claim that the language of metaphysics, when redefined so as to disengage it from its traditional abuses, has as its task 'to organise the supply of all these supplementary words [of science and history] and at the same time to collect the simplest possible number of them to fulfil their task as ultimate co-ordinates, and then to offer the resultant group as a sort of index to the total language scheme, which comprises both the index and the subordinate languages with their several logics'.[74]

And now for the relevance of all this to Ramsey's view of religious experience! He is convinced that the linguistic necessity of such metaphysical terms and language indicates an experiential necessity as well.[75] Even as the languages of science and history arose as a methodological response for dealing with certain aspects of reality, so the language of what P. F. Strawson has termed 'descriptive metaphysics' has evolved as part of the fabric of human discourse in order to enable people to respond to, and discuss, other important aspects of reality. In particular, Ramsey thinks that the terms 'activity', 'I', 'person', and 'God' can all be shown to function as vehicles for expressing disclosures of experiential reality which cannot be handled in the more object-centred languages.[76] All of this can be seen to relate quite clearly to Ramsey's overall position concerning disclosures which was discussed in Section One of this chapter.

It is in connection with such metaphysical language, reflecting as it does discernments and commitments which arise from within, but go beyond empirical facts, that the concept of miracle finds its

73

logical location and its religious significance. Ramsey sets forth two
defining characteristics of a miracle: it must be an event which both
fails to conform to the uniform pattern of scientific description, and
which functions as a medium of such power and goodness that it
demands to be discussed in terms of such metaphysical language as
'God's activity'.[77] Elsewhere he combines these characteristics in
the form of a definition: 'Miracle is a particular configuration of
events giving rise to a disclosure on the basis of which we use the
language of personal decisive activity about God.'[78] As far as I can
tell, Ramsey means to present each of these two characteristics as
necessary, but not sufficient, conditions for calling an event 'a
miracle'. The fulfilment of the first apart from the second is simply
an oddity, while the fulfilment of the second apart from the first
is best described in terms of 'providence'.[79]

After summarising his position in terms of a distinction between
'first-order activity' (described by scientific language) and 'second-
order activity' (disclosures necessitating talk about 'persons' and
'I'), Ramsey concludes by suggesting that:

'. . . the word "miracle" is a word in the logic of (metaphysical)
history which is used to describe an event which witnesses to,
and is an occasion of, a *personal, second-order* activity of God,
of which we are in some basic and non-inferential sense directly
aware. A miracle is an historical event which, *a fortiori* demand-
ing for its description "personal activity", needs also the description "God". The difficulty of mapping the word "miracle", is,
then, precisely the difficulty of having the words "personal
activity" *and* the word "God" used of an event treated his-
torically.'[80]

In other words, the concept of miracle is to be located in the context
of historical language, as opposed to scientific language, as the
former is 'bounded' by metaphysical terms such as 'personal activity'
and 'God'.

Finally, on Ramsey's account, to say that a miracle occurred is:
(1) to maintain that a particular event (M) has provided a broader
and deeper understanding of related past and contemporary events;
(2) to commend a particular metaphysical language index involving
locutions containing the term 'God', which will serve to relate historical language and all other language-games more adequately than
other metaphysical languages; (3) to assert that the particular event
in question (M) took place within an empirical situation which

74

included a 'non-inferential awareness' (disclosure) that was not any less real for not being reducible to language about first-order activity.[81] All of these assertions are involved in making the claim that 'God's second-order (or personal) activity' was present in (M).

On the basis of this general analysis of Ramsey's interpretation of miracles, it can be seen that he views miracles as a special case of disclosure-commitment situations which reveal a religious dimension of experience and reality. While some disclosures occur in connection with concepts, moral obligation, personal relations, and the like, those which are called miracles occur in connection with historical events. Once again it is important to emphasise the fact that Ramsey does not view religious disclosures in general, or miraculous disclosures in particular, as discontinuous with the rest of human experience. Indeed, he constantly seeks to trace the experiential and logical connections between religious and non-religious experience, by way of avoiding the opposing pitfalls of a narrow naturalism on the one hand and a wild supernaturalism on the other. Natural experience is more mysterious, and religious experience less mysterious, than the advocates of either are often willing to admit!

In another essay Ramsey addresses himself more specifically to the question of the resurrection of Jesus Christ, and an examination of his comments in that connection will serve to focus and underline the main themes of both his concept of miracle and his interpretation of religious disclosure. Once again, the general theme of Ramsey's approach is clearly expressed in the broad thesis of the particular essay. At the outset he makes it clear that in his view, although it clearly involves the matter-of-fact dimension, '. . . resurrection-belief is something more than belief in a matter of fact. . . .'[82]

Ramsey begins by analysing three resurrection passages in the New Testament by way of elucidating his claim that belief in the resurrection involves belief in certain facts and more. First, he discusses the story of the two disciples on the road to Emmaus. In a sense, the one who traced the resurrection theme in the Old Testament for these disciples was simply another person recounting some facts. And yet at a certain point in his seemingly routine behaviour (giving thanks for the meal), these disciples discerned that this one was the same Jesus they had known before his death. Moreover, Ramsey thinks it is extremely significant that during the experience the hearts of these men 'glowed within them', and after their discernment of the risen Christ they connected this subjective experience with the objective disclosure. Ramsey feels that this fact points up the important mediational value of self-awareness in relation to religious disclosure.

Second, he examines the story of 'doubting Thomas'. Here the concern for empirical grounding is clearly displayed in Thomas's refusal to believe until he could see and touch, and thus identify, the risen Lord. Nevertheless, when the empirical evidence is offered, Thomas discerns far more in the situation than nail-holes, flesh and blood. The facts involved came together in such a way as to enable Thomas to ascertain their cosmic dimension, and he expressed this discernment in his total commitment, 'My Lord and my God'.

Third, the same general pattern can be seen in the account of Christ's appearance to Mary at the empty tomb. The significance of the empty tomb, in relation to her past experience of the person of Jesus, did not 'dawn on' Mary at first. Even when Christ appeared to her she mistook him for a gardener! Only when he called her by name did she discern the significance of this strange pattern of events. Here again, Ramsey is impressed with the crucial, mediational role played by the introduction of the personal dimension in the form of a personal name.

Ramsey summarises[83] the main elements involved in the discernment of miracle in general, and of the Resurrection in particular. The similarity between these elements and those discussed earlier on will be obvious. Furthermore, Ramsey indicates that the pattern of contemporary Resurrection-belief is essentially the same, although today the factual elements are historical rather than sensory. First, there are always certain matters of fact which, whether they are sensory or historical, serve as the empirical anchor for the discernment of a miracle. Such matters of fact relate the disclosure to public events in such a way as to guard against hallucination and fraud. Although the reality of a discernment cannot be strictly deduced from these facts, there is a sense in which they do provide some degree of verification. This aspect of Ramsey's thought will be discussed in Chapter Five. All that can be said at this point is that the objective element involved in a discernment is as real as that involved in the knowledge of other persons, although in neither case is this reality strictly deduced or inferred from empirical facts.

The second element involved in Ramsey's understanding of the discernment of miracles is the disclosure of a dimension whose significance supersedes that of empirical facts. This is what religious people refer to as 'the activity of God', and it comprises a significant aspect of what is usually termed religious experience. This discernment is similar to becoming aware of the love and activity of a personal friend by means of his words and behaviour. Third, Ramsey calls attention to the response of commitment which arises out of such a discernment-situation. This element is also clearly seen in each of the Resurrection narratives discussed above. It is clearly an essential aspect of all religious experience.

After thus analysing and summarising the distinctive character of Resurrection-belief in relation to the overall logic of the concept of miracle, Ramsey concludes by re-emphasising the essential connection between the facts and the disclosure involved in a disclosure-situation.

'But in emphasising the distinctive character of the Christian belief in the Resurrection, it has been no part of my purpose to deny its essential reference to "objects of sense" as well. Indeed, on the contrary, I have tried to give a hint about how the two points can be combined, about how the logical gap can be bridged. The hint comes from recognising what has likewise to be both distinguished and related in situations of human love and devotion. For here, too, there are "objects of sense" and more. Characteristically, personal behaviour is more than "what's seen" . . . we shall be helped to meet . . . criticism if we concentrate on this personal model, and in particular if we develop the theme that while of course all personal loyalty is anchored in some facts of an empirical kind, personal devotion never builds on empirical fact with a nicely calculated less or more.'[84]

This then is how Ramsey's view of disclosure-commitment experience informs his understanding of miracles. Along with disclosures of freedom and immortality, disclosures of God's activity seem to go beyond cosmic disclosures in that they focus more on self-knowledge and are more specific in their content. In contrast to disclosures of freedom and immortality, however, disclosures of God's activity are more closely related to the events of history and inter-personal activity. Nevertheless, all forms of religious disclosure are seen to follow the broad pattern of a commitment to a discernment which arises out of a particular empirical setting. Moreover, religious disclosures are in many ways continuous with the more common disclosures of the linguistic, perceptual, conceptual, moral, and personal dimensions. Indeed, the religious dimension is mediated through these other dimensions.

In this chapter I have examined the main aspects of Ramsey's

Ian Ramsey

understanding of religious experience by focusing on his concept of the disclosure-situation. In the next chapter I shall examine his interpretation of the language which religious people use to talk about their religious disclosures in general, and about their disclosures of God in particular.

NOTES

1 Ian Ramsey, 'Towards the Relevant in Theological Language', *Modern Churchman*, VIII (September 1964), pp. 47.

2 Ramsey, 'On Understanding Mystery', *Chicago Theological Seminary Register*, LIII, no. 5 (May 1963), p. 3. Also in *Christian Empiricism*, p. 64.

3 Ramsey, 'Contemporary Empiricism', *The Christian Scholar*, XLIII, no. 3 (Fall 1960), p. 181. Also in *Christian Empiricism*, p. 12.

4 'Contemporary Empiricism', p. 176. Also in *Christian Empiricism*, p. 6.

5 'On Understanding Mystery', p. 1. Also in *Christian Empiricism*, p. 59.

6 John Hick, *Faith and Knowledge*, esp. Chapter 6.

7 St Thomas Aquinas, *Summa Theologica*, Part I, Question 13.

8 Joseph Butler, *The Analogy of Religion*, Introduction and Part I.

9 Ramsey, *Religious Language*.

10 ibid., p. 19.

11 Unfortunately, these remarks have not been published, but I do have a tape recording of the discussion which serves to document the above comments. A similar point is made in *Religious Language*, p. 62.

12 *Religious Language*, pp. 25–6.

13 Ludwig Wittgenstein, *Philosophical Investigations*, trans. G. E. M. Anscombe, Part 2, pp. 193–214.

14 *Religious Language*, pp. 35–6.

15 ibid., pp. 78–9.

16 'Religion and Science: A Philosopher's Approach', *Church Quarterly Review*, CLXII (January–March 1961), pp. 77ff. Also in *Christian Empiricism*, pp. 140ff.

17 *Religious Language*, pp. 33–4, 47–9.

18 'Ethics and Reason', *Church Quarterly Review*, CLVIII (April–June 1957), pp. 153ff. Also in *Christian Empiricism*, pp. 48ff.

19 Ramsey (ed.), *Prospect for Metaphysics*, Chapter 10.

20 ibid., p. 171.

21 *Religious Language*, pp. 17–18.

22 Cf. ibid., p. 23.

23 Gilbert Ryle, *The Concept of Mind*, and P. F. Strawson, 'Persons', *The Philosophy of Mind*, ed. V. C. Chappell, Chapter 7. Wittgenstein said something similar to this in his *Philosophical Investigations*, p. 178.

24 For a more thorough discussion of the relation of Ramsey's thought to that of Ryle and Strawson, see his 'Biology and Personality', *Philosophical Forum*, XXI (1964), p. 32. Also in *Christian Empiricism*, pp. 32–47.

25 *Prospect for Metaphysics*, pp. 169–170.

26 'Towards the Relevant in Theological Language', p. 50. Perhaps it should be noted that Ramsey never opts for such phrases as 'dis-

embodied soul' or 'ghost in a machine' to talk of the transcendent referent of such terms.

27 'On Understanding Mystery', p. 4. Also in *Christian Empiricism*, p. 63.
28 This is even evident in David Hume's ironic conclusion, to the effect that *'I have no experience of a self'*. Cf. David Hume, *A Treatise of Human Nature*, Part II.
29 'On Understanding Mystery', p. 4. Also in *Christian Empiricism*, p. 64.
30 ibid., p. 5; *Christian Empiricism*, p. 64.
31 ibid., pp. 4–5; *Christian Empiricism*, p. 64.
32 'On Understanding Mystery', p. 5; *Christian Empiricism*, p. 65.
33 *Prospect for Metaphysics*, p. 167.
34 *Religious Language*, pp. 24–5.
35 'On Understanding Mystery', p. 6; *Christian Empiricism*, p. 66.
36 *Prospect for Metaphysics*, pp. 172–3. This idea is also expressed in some unpublished notes of Ramsey's on the 'Philosophy of Religion'.
37 'Towards the Relevant in Theological Language', p. 50. Cf. also 'On Understanding Mystery', p. 6, and *Prospect for Metaphysics*, p. 173.
38 Ramsey, 'Some Further Reflections on "Freedom and Immortality" ', *Hibbert Journal*, LIX (July 1961), p. 355. Also in *Christian Empiricism*, p. 228.
39 *Religious Language*, p. 39.
40 ibid., p. 53.
41 *Freedom and Immortality*, Chapter 1.
42 Cf. John L. Austin, *Philosophical Papers*, p. 130.
43 *Freedom and Immortality*, p. 26.
44 ibid., p. 26.
45 ibid., p. 38.
46 ibid., pp. 39ff.
47 ibid., pp. 30–1.
48 ibid., pp. 42–3.
49 This discussion is contained in letters written by Bertrand Russell and A. J. Ayer to the *Observer*, on 13 and 20 October 1957.
50 *Freedom and Immortality*, p. 44.
51 ibid., p. 48.
52 ibid., p. 49.
53 ibid., p. 53.
54 Ramsey (ed.), *Christian Ethics and Contemporary Philosophy*, Chapter 9.
55 *Freedom and Immortality*, pp. 61ff.
56 ibid., p. 66.
57 ibid., p. 67.
58 ibid., p. 74.
59 ibid., p. 81.
60 ibid., p. 82.
61 ibid., pp. 83–8.
62 ibid., p. 111.
63 ibid., pp. 113–48.
64 ibid., p. 151.
65 Anthony Flew, 'Can a Man Witness His Own Funeral?' *Hibbert Journal*, LIV (April 1956), pp. 242.
66 Ramsey, 'Persons and Funerals: What Do Person Words Mean?', *Hibbert Journal*, LIV (June 1956), p. 336.

67 Ramsey *et al.*, *The Miracles and the Resurrection*, p. 3.
68 ibid., pp. 4–5. Many of these same features are discussed in Ramsey's 'Religion and Science: A Philosopher's Approach'. This article will be discussed in detail in Chapter 5.
69 ibid., p. 7.
70 ibid., pp. 7–8.
71 ibid., p. 8.
72 ibid., pp. 11–12.
73 ibid., p. 13.
74 ibid., p. 15.
75 ibid., p. 17.
76 ibid., p. 21.
77 ibid., p. 21.
78 Cf. page 29 of Ramsey's unpublished notes on the 'Philosophy of Religion'.
79 *The Miracles and the Resurrection*, pp. 22–5.
80 ibid., p. 25.
81 ibid., p. 27. This same point is brought out in *Religious Language*, pp. 167–74, especially p. 174.
82 Ramsey, 'The Logical Character of Resurrection-belief', *Theology*, LX, no. 443 (May 1957), p. 188. Also in *Christian Empiricism*, p. 179.
83 ibid., p. 191; *Christian Empiricism*, p. 182.
84 ibid., p. 192; *Christian Empiricism*, p. 184.

Chapter 4

THE FUNCTION OF CHRISTIAN GOD-TALK

On the final page of *Freedom and Immortality*, Ramsey sets forth three convictions which lie behind his arguments concerning the nature of talk about freedom and immortality. It is not inappropriate to suggest that these convictions underlie Ramsey's interpretations of the rest of religious discourse as well. The first conviction is that the vast and complex diversity of ordinary language leaves room for the possibility of speaking about the 'unseen' aspect of human experience. The second is that theological language must be understood as an attempt to express the twofold nature of religious experience—namely its observable dimension and its non-observable dimension. Third, many of the problems involved in the attempt to understand religious language arise from a failure to discern the logic of its two-dimensional thrust.

Ramsey concludes his convictional confession with the following reflection:

'None of these convictions is in itself very startling or novel, but at least they register a protest against two popular misconceptions: that those with an intense affection for ordinary language must necessarily deny metaphysics, or that those who defend metaphysics must necessarily trade in occult realms and shadowy worlds. Which means that the book has been fighting on two battle-fronts at once; and it is a sobering reflection that not many wars have been won under such a necessity.'[1]

I propose to use these three convictions as the pegs upon which to hang the considerations of this present chapter. The first section will deal with the logical oddness of both ordinary and religious language. The second will focus on the specific nature of Christian God-talk in terms of Ramsey's concepts of 'models' and 'qualifiers'. The third will trace Ramsey's application of his interpretation to biblical and theological language, including the language of paradox. I shall conclude the chapter with a brief account of Ramsey's claim that the term 'God' functions as an 'integrative term'.

1 LOGICAL ODDNESS

Oddness is a relative concept. What is odd in relationship to one aspect of experience is often commonplace with respect to another, and vice versa. This is a point which is frequently overlooked by those who dismiss religious language as cognitively meaningless on the basis of the fact that in relationship to scientific language it seems to be 'logically odd'. This is one of Ramsey's most often repeated criticisms. Only when the straightforward, empirical language of science is taken as normative is it possible to dismiss religious discourse as an oddity. When viewed against the broader background of ordinary language, religious language does not appear at all out of place. Indeed, there are even aspects of scientific discourse which are quite odd, either in relationship to strict sensory reports on the one hand, or in relationship to ordinary language on the other hand. It is in connection with this aspect of Ramsey's thought that the influence of Wittgenstein becomes explicitly apparent. It is in this sense that Ramsey is to be classified as an ordinary language philosopher.

The criterion for judging the appropriateness or inappropriateness of various locutions is their adequacy for dealing with the dimension of experience in which they find their home. If religious language is going to do justice to the complex nature of religious experience, as discussed in Chapter Three, then it must necessarily exhibit a rather complex logic.

'Our broad conclusion [is] that if this discernment-commitment is the kind of situation characteristic of religion, we must expect religious language to be appropriately odd, and to have a distinctive logical behaviour. Otherwise it would not be currency for the strange kind of situation about which it claims to speak.'[2]

Throughout his writings Ramsey bases his case for the logical oddness of God-talk upon the peculiarities inherent in the logic of the first-person pronoun 'I'. Following the lead of Wittgenstein and other philosophers of language, Ramsey takes the distinction between the two main uses of 'I' to be of special significance.[3] Going beyond these philosophers, Ramsey finds in this distinction a paradigm case of a locution which exhibits a two-dimensional nature. That is, the term 'I' can be used by the speaker to refer to himself, and as a vehicle to express his statements. This two-dimensional nature of the term 'I', which will be discussed in detail shortly, is, according to Ramsey, similar to that of Christian God-talk, for both are attempts to deal with the disclosure-situation out of which they arise. This similarity is especially significant with respect to Ramsey's claim that religious disclosures are often mediated through a disclosure of self-awareness.

With respect to the question of the oddness of God-talk, it is important to note the special significance of the oddness of first person-talk. Here is a case of a locution which in reference to object-talk is exceedingly odd, but which in reference to everyday language is exceedingly ordinary. In fact, it could be argued that, without the two-dimensional thrust of the term 'I', human discourse would be impossible. As Ramsey says, 'odd language may well have a distinctive significance, and we might even conclude in the end that the odder the language the more it matters to us'.[4]

Although this theme of the logical oddness of the term 'I' runs through all of Ramsey's writings, it is most thoroughly treated in his article entitled 'The Systematic Elusiveness of "I" '.[5] For this reason I shall focus upon this article for the remainder of this section, occasionally drawing upon other sources as well. The major conclusion which Ramsey draws from all his discussions of this subject is that there are aspects of experience which cannot be exhausted in terms of observables, and that the language about these aspects cannot be reduced to talk about observables. This is, of course, not to say that such talk could ever be completely divorced from talk about observables. It is the commonness and importance of such talk, especially in the case of the first person pronoun, that Ramsey thinks provides the foundation for language about God.

Ramsey begins his discussion of 'The Systematic Elusiveness of "I" ' by tracing the difficulties which David Hume encountered while trying to pin down the logic of self-awareness and personal identity.[6] Since the only epistemological objects Hume would accept were sense impressions, and since one could never obtain a sense impression of one's self, Hume concluded that the concepts of self-hood and personal identity are bogus. However, since people (including Hume himself) found the concept indispensable, both practically and theoretically, he remained dissatisfied with his analytic conclusion. Setting aside the many difficulties connected with Hume's assumption concerning sense impressions, Ramsey calls attention to the fact that the very notion of an epistemological 'object' implies the existence of a corresponding 'subject'. In the final analysis, no account of experience in terms of objects alone can ever exhaust the knowing situation, since each such account must be made by a knowing subject.[7]

Next, Ramsey traces Gilbert Ryle's attempt to solve Hume's dilemma in terms of 'higher order actions'.[8] Ryle maintains that statements involving references to oneself, such as 'I am running', fail to encompass their own subject-dimension, but that this subject-dimension can be encompassed by a second statement of a higher order, such as 'I said "I am running" '. Although this second statement leaves its own subject-dimension unencompassed, it is possible to represent this higher order activity in yet a third statement, and so on, *ad infinitum*. Thus, even though no particular statement involving a self-reference is ever complete, Ryle concludes that there is nothing mysterious involved. Self-references are systematically elusive, but can be 'captured' by means of a higher order statement. Ramsey agrees with much of what Ryle sets forth, but insists that more needs to be, and can be, said.

The main objection which Ramsey raises against the views of Hume and Ryle is aimed at what he takes to be their common basic assumption. He claims that both thinkers maintain 'that any situation which becomes the "object" of a higher order action is unchanged in the process'.[9] In other words, the assumption which Ramsey challenges is that there is no difference between the 'I' which is unsaid in the statement 'I am running' and the first 'I' in the statement 'I said "I am running" '. He maintains that an essential change has taken place when the 'speaking "I" ' has been objectified by a higher order statement.

The negative reasons for Ramsey's rejection of this assumption derive from the major problems which it leaves unanswered. First, as was mentioned in connection with the above reference to Hume, this assumption ignores the subject-object distinction which is necessary to every knowing situation, and thereby makes it impossible to say anything about the subject dimension of experience in the present.

'If we assume that what eludes us now becomes in the next minute wholly tractable, then since, at this next minute, an earlier situation has been completely objectified, what account can we then give of the subject-object distinction which is the permanent pre-supposition of all living and talking alike? What account can we give of our "subjectivity" "now"?'[10]

Using Ryle's example by way of illustrating the difficulty raised by this assumption, Ramsey points out that such a view places the 'I' on the same epistemological level as the 'myself' in the statement, 'I was laughing at myself for being butter-fingered'. Ramsey contends that prior to proceeding to a second-order description of this statement, something is known experientially and implied linguistically about the subject when and as he makes the statement! To assume that nothing is lost when moving from a first-order to a second-order statement involving self-reference is to raise havoc with the epistemological context of everyday experience.

Another related difficulty, raised by the assumption Ramsey attacks, concerns the problem of personal identity. If first person references are always to be either eliminated or translated to the object level by means of higher order statements, what is it that is to supply the continuity between the subject-speaker of the original statement and the objectified 'I' of the second statement? In Ramsey's terms:

'The formula is meant to make it plain that any attempt by "I" to discover "I" replaces "I" by some I_n and so on without end. So the problem of "personal identity" is now raised in this way, viz. How are we to talk of "one self" if all we have is an infinite series of perceptual terms?'[11]

The force of this objection is clearly seen when one recalls the overwhelming significance and commonness of the 'proto-concept' of personal identity in everyday experience and language. Any view which fails to provide a basis for personal continuity leaves a good deal to be desired.

The positive aspect of Ramsey's argument is twofold.[12] First, he is concerned to display, or evoke, an understanding of the logic and implications of the term 'I'. The terms 'display' and 'evoke' are chosen deliberately in order to emphasise Ramsey's acknowledgement that this type of understanding cannot be set forth as a description in terms of straightforward, observational language. Rather, he attempts to sketch actual and imaginary situations in human experience which will give rise to an explicit acknowledgement of that of which all men are tacitly aware—namely that they are selves which cannot be exhaustively described in terms of public behaviour. The situations which Ramsey makes use of in this context are very similar to those discussed in the section on disclosures in Chapter Three. Neither changes in size, appearance, nor behaviour, whether gradual or sudden, slight or extreme, ever cause the person involved to become confused about his own identity. Nor can violent psychological disruptions induced by experimental drugs or loss of memory ever cause the person involved to doubt his own self-hood. Thus there is an important, indeed absolutely essential, dimension of human experience implied in the 'subject-use' of the first person pronoun which cannot be accounted for by reference to higher order actions and statements. The necessity of an epistemological subject which is aware of its own identity is implied in the subject-use of 'I'.

The second positive aspect of Ramsey's twofold argument involves the drawing of parallels between the oddness of 'I' and such terms as 'feeling' and 'action'.[13] These latter terms can be used in such a way as to permit assimilation to the level of object-talk, but they can also be used in ways which do not permit such assimilation. We all talk of having certain feelings, such as 'apprehension', and performing certain actions, such as 'making up our mind', that, although they are related to behavioural patterns, cannot be reduced to such patterns. Ramsey concludes that such terms, like 'I', are simply logically odd, and ought to be recognised as such. Moreover, this logical oddness can be seen to be integrally related to the reality of self-awareness as outlined above.

Ramsey is especially concerned to dissociate his view from those which argue for the existence of a metaphysical or 'transcendental' self. The way in which the term 'I' expresses the reality of the self is similar to the way in which the term 'infinite sum' expresses the reality of a particular mathematical function. In neither case is anything occult being introduced. In each case an essential posit of the appropriate 'language-game' or 'form of life' is being put to use. Nor does Ramsey's approach commit him to a view which implies that the knowing-subject has some form of 'privileged access', such as a 'private language' or isolated awareness. Indeed, one of the main thrusts of Ramsey's interpretation is that the self-awareness which each person possesses is mediated by means of inter-personal relationships and discourse.[14]

Ramsey's own summary of the experiential and linguistic conclusion of his argument is extremely pointed:

'Summarising then, we may say that the systematic elusiveness of 'I' relates to the *fact* that self-awareness, as characterising highest order "actions," or "feelings" of personal identity, cannot be adequately dealt with in terms of those elements to which a highest order action *objectively* refers and which become available for treatment later. . . . From the point of view of *language*, the systematic elusiveness of "I" makes the claim that "I" systematically eludes all observation language; it is a claim that "I" has a logical status all of its own and is not a "perception" word. Perhaps, indeed . . . we have here a starting point for an empirically based and suitably chastened metaphysics. But that would be another story.'[15]

It is on the basis of this analysis of the logical oddness of 'I' that Ramsey goes on to build his 'other story' concerning Christian God-talk. If 'I', although logically odd, is appropriate currency for self-awareness, then perhaps 'God', although logically odd, is appropriate currency for religious awareness!

2 MODELS AND QUALIFIERS

The most thorough treatment that Ramsey gives of the precise nature of God-talk is found in the second chapter of his *Religious Language*, and this will serve as the primary source for the present discussion. Other pertinent material will be referred to as well.

It is absolutely essential to see the correspondence which Ramsey constructs between his understanding of religious experience and his interpretation of talk about God. The twofold nature of religious discourse, involving both the perceptual and religious dimension, is matched by the twofold thrust of religious language. Ramsey's essential thesis is that religious locutions, especially those in which the the term 'God' is employed, exhibit a concern for both the perceptual and the 'unseen' (but none the less real) dimensions of experience. The former concern is expressed by means of what Ramsey terms 'models', while the latter concern is expressed by means of what Ramsey calls 'qualifiers'.

By the term 'model', Ramsey means to designate that aspect of religious discourse which serves to call attention to the factual elements that mediate religious disclosure.[16] In any given disclosure-situation, certain empirical elements come together in such a way as to reveal a dimension which encompasses, but goes beyond these elements themselves. With respect to religious disclosures, the language which gains currency preserves the mediational connection between these two dimensions by employing a 'model' term, or phrase, which serves to anchor the religious expression, and thus the religious experience, in everyday empirical experience.

By the term 'qualifier', Ramsey means to designate that aspect of religious discourse which serves to call attention to the fact that the dimension which is revealed in a disclosure-situation cannot be equated with the empirical elements that mediate it.[17] In other words, the qualifier-term in a religious locution functions as a warning that the model-term is not to be interpreted in a simple, straightforward fashion. The qualifier-term points beyond the empirical model in order to indicate that there is an 'unseen' dimension of the experience in question. In addition, Ramsey asserts that the qualifier-term also provides a clue concerning how the model-term is to be developed by way of disclosing the deeper dimension.[18]

The juxtaposition of these two aspects of religious discourse thus provides a bridge between empirical experience and language on the one hand, and religious experience and language on the other. One is neither limited to talking about God in exclusively empirical terms (anthropomorphic univocation) nor forced to talk of Him in non-empirical terms (metaphysical equivocation). Metaphysical presuppositions aside, the obvious similarities between Ramsey's approach to theological language and that of St Thomas Aquinas make it clear that, in a broad sense, Ramsey's position is to be classified as one that follows the 'middle way' of analogy.

> 'The overall lesson to be learned, then, is that if we want to understand language which claims to talk of a mystery, if we want to understand some piece of distinctive religious discourse, we must first pick out the words which are most straightforward and most obviously descriptive. We then look at the other words to see which of them act as qualifiers behaving logically like an imperative to direct us to a disclosure. Every complete religious assertion will thus use words descriptively and also specify a technique by which we may move from "what is seen" to "what is seen and more", from the expressible to the point where the expressible becomes part of the inexpressible.'[19]

The foregoing abstract definition of Ramsey's key concepts will be greatly clarified by an examination of the specific examples he uses to illustrate how these concepts function with respect to some

traditional characterisations of God. He divides these characterisations into three kinds, and discusses several examples of each. The
first two kinds make use of the 'model-qualifier' pattern implicitly,
while the third makes use of it explicitly. Ramsey's classifications
are: (1) the attributes of negative theology, (2) the one-word
attributes of positive characterisation, and (3) the two-word attributes of positive characterisation.

The suggestion with regard to negative attributes is that they are
to be interpreted as focusing on that aspect of experience which does
not participate in the change and fluctuation of everyday experience,
but which, rather, is the very thing which holds the changing aspects
of experience together as unity.[20] In other words, negative characterisations of God, such as 'God is immutable', are attempts to call
attention to that aspect of experience which provides the continuity or structure of any and all experience. Obviously, it is
difficult, if not impossible, to give positive labels to this element of
experience which one has discerned. This is the reason that
characterisations of such discernments take a negative, and thus
logically odd, form. 'Mutable' serves as the model in this characterisation, and 'im-' as the negative qualifier.

Perhaps the most illuminating illustration which Ramsey gives
of this type of discourse is in his analysis of what takes place when
one is confronted with an old friend whom he has not seen for
many years. Clearly much, if not most, has changed. Yet, not
everything has changed, and it is this discernment which causes one
to say, for example, 'He is still the same', or 'He hasn't really
changed'. Thus it is that negative descriptions of God can function
as symbols of that which has been discerned as unchanging in our
experience. In addition, the main function of using such terms is not
to describe God scientifically, but to evoke a situation in which
one will be able to discern this peculiar aspect of experience. Here
is Ramsey's own summary of this discussion:

> 'So when we talk of God as "immutable", or as "impassible",
> the function of these particular attribute-words is primarily to
> evoke the kind of situation we have just been mentioning; to fix
> on mutable and passible features of perceptual situations and
> to develop these features in such a way that there is evoked a
> characteristically different situation which is the foundation *in
> fact* for assertions about God's immutability or impassibility. But
> there is a little more to it than that. For these words "immuta-
> bility" and "impassibility" make also a *language* plea. They

89

claim for the word "God" a position outside all mutable and passible language. Beyond that negative claim the attributes of negative theology do not however go. All they tell us is that if anything is "mutable" it will not be exact currency for God; that if anything is "passible" it will not be exact currency for God. So the main merit of attribute words like "immutable" and "impassible" is to give a kind of technique for meditation; their main merit is evocative.'[21]

Positive characterisations of God which make use of only one word can be best understood, according to Ramsey, as attempts to describe God by means of the method of contrasts.[22] Such terms as 'unity', 'simplicity', and 'perfection' are suggested as examples of the use of this method in talking of God. 'Unity' is used to call attention to the discernment that often arises out of an exposure to the diversity of experience. Such is the case in the understanding and use of class, or set, theory, and also in the experiences evoked by experiments in Gestalt psychology.

The same is said to hold true with regard to the use of 'simplicity' and 'perfection'. This latter term is of special interest because of its importance throughout the history of philosophical and religious thought. Ramsey feels that one learns the use of terms like 'perfection' by inductively examining various imperfect aspects of experience, and ordering them according to their decreasing imperfection until 'the penny drops' and one discerns what is meant. It is clear that such terms do not point to some unseen, Platonic form, or to a mental picture. None the less, the experience of learning how to use such terms clearly involves a discernment of some aspect of experience which is no less real for being mental. Ramsey concludes his consideration of this type of characterisation of God by suggesting that 'perfection' functions in a way very similar to the concept of a limit in mathematics.[23]

The last group of characterisations, those that use two words to give a positive prediction of God, is thought by Ramsey to be the most illuminating with regard to both the empirical ground and logical oddity of religious language.[24] He deals with five examples: 'first cause', 'infinitely wise', 'infinitely good', 'creation out of nothing', and 'eternal purpose'.

The pattern of such terms is twofold. First, the words 'cause', 'wise', 'good', 'creation', 'purpose', and others like them, function as models. That is, a term is used to designate a situation with which people are generally acquainted in experience. It brings to mind examples of causal relations, wise people, good people and situations, making things, human purposes, and the like. A model thus serves to anchor these theological phrases in 'a situation with which we are all familiar, and which can be used for reaching another situation with which we are not so familiar; one which, without the model, we should not recognise so easily'.[25]

Second, the words 'first', 'infinite', 'out-of-nothing', and 'eternal' function as qualifiers. These qualifiers have at least two separate functions,[26] namely, (1) to indicate in which direction the models are to be developed, and (2) to express the logical limitations of the model term when used in connection with God. The function of indicating the direction in which to develop a particular model has to do with suggesting that, when used in discourse about God, words like 'cause', 'wise', and 'good' are to be developed in the direction of their higher degrees. This would seem to be a type of 'analogical pointer' in that one is saying 'Begin here and move in that direction'. Such a 'pointer' is not to be mistaken for a description of the destination.

The function of expressing the logical limitations of model terms by means of such logical qualifiers also needs further explanation. Ramsey likens this function of qualifiers to that of terms like 'infinite' in conjunction with 'sum' in the language of mathematics. Although the phrase 'infinite sum' may have the same verbal grammar as such phrases as 'large sum' and 'small sum', it has a distinctively different logic. No specific sum can ever be given. ' "Infinite" then, as a theologian would use it, is not at all unlike its use in mathematics in relation to generated sequences for which a word of odd logic is posited at the end in relation to what could be called "mathematical insight" '.[27] In like manner, such phrases as 'infinitely good' and 'eternal purpose' have the same verbal grammar as 'very good' and 'long range purpose' respectively, but their logic is very different. The terms 'good' and 'purpose' need this sort of qualification if they are to function as models rather than anthropomorphisms.

The point is stressed often in Ramsey's writings that in no sense are the characterisations of God in religious language to be taken as metaphysical or psychological descriptions. These characterisations are much more akin to the language of metaphor and parable which, incidentally, pervades even our mathematical and scientific language, to say nothing of ordinary discourse. When one discerns a new relationship, in any area of experience, which does not quite fit into previous categories, new words are coined, or words are borrowed from other areas of experience, in order to express this new 'disclosure'. These new or borrowed words often take on a logic of their own. Much confusion has resulted from the failure of theologians and philosophers to pay sufficient attention to the logical oddness of religious characterisations of God. Ramsey devotes a good deal of space to showing how many of the puzzles and difficulties in the history of philosophical theology can be avoided by applying the foregoing analysis of religious language.[28]

In his essay 'On Understanding Mystery', Ramsey makes some summary remarks about the logical nature of this model-qualifier schema.[29] First, in order to avoid confusions and false problems, religious assertions should always be so formulated as to include both a model-term and a qualifier-term. Such statements as 'God is love', 'God exists', and 'God is the Father' ought to be appropriately qualified by such terms as 'infinite', 'necessary', and 'Heavenly' respectively. Without such qualifications, these assertions and others like them are extremely likely to be taken as straightforward, empirical assertions. In like manner, it is obvious that religious assertions which fail to anchor themselves in empirical experience by means of a model-term are at best misleading, and at worst cognitively empty. Qualifiers cannot function independently of other terms. Simply to say, for example, 'God is infinite' or 'God is necessary' is to say very little indeed!

Second, although it is the model-terms which provide the content of religious assertions, Ramsey insists that it must never be thought that such terms are exhaustively articulate concerning that to which they refer. Models are, after all, only models! This fact necessitates that new models be sought and constructed constantly. New models are needed to offset the misleading implications that might derive from trying to make any given model 'walk on all fours'. A variety of models provides a helpful system of 'checks and balances'. Moreover, new models may actually increase our knowledge of God, at least within a given historical context. This bringing together of more than one model actually functions as a form of qualification.

Third, Ramsey admits that what takes place when a disclosure breaks in on a person, and thereby gives rise to a response of commitment, involves some sort of 'logical leap' and necessary risk. The disclosure and its corresponding commitment do not follow from the empirical facts the way a conclusion follows from the premises in a syllogistic argument. Ramsey sees a similarity between his concept of 'revelation by disclosure and commitment' and Kierkegaard's 'leap of faith'. However, he is quick to point out

92

that, in his understanding, the leap of commitment is less fore-boding because both the destination and the take-off platform are more continuous with the rest of human experience than they were for Kierkegaard.[30] Moreover there is a sense, for both Ramsey and Kierkegaard, in which the 'leap' is actually more of a 'being carried over', since there is no way to guarantee its success.

In connection with his discussion of the model-qualifier pattern of Christian God-talk, Ramsey undertakes a brief application of this pattern to the traditional problem of evil. It will be profitable to examine his discussion of this subject by way of coming to a clearer understanding of the model-qualifier pattern. A more thorough analysis of Ramsey's application of this pattern to biblical and theological language will be taken up in the next section.

After rejecting those approaches which attempt to avoid the problem by denying either the reality of evil or the full perfection of God, Ramsey suggests that each of the traditional theological approaches to the problem can be seen to make an important con-tribution, if it is understood in terms of the model-qualifier schema.[31] This is a case of balancing one model with yet other models so as to develop a 'multi-model' discourse. The moves which introduce talk about 'the fall', God's 'permissive will', God's 'self-limitation', and God's 'purposive, redemptive love' are all seen in their best light when viewed as instances of models which qualify one another.[32] Each one builds upon some familiar aspect of human experience, and qualifies it by combining it with other aspects. The attempt is to bring together these various aspects in such a way as to incorporate instances of evil while giving rise to a disclosure of a way in which God's relation to the world can be grasped in a balanced pattern. Although Ramsey thinks there is value in each of these traditional approaches when they are com-bined in a multi-model discourse, he is convinced that the approach employing talk of redemptive and purposive love, deriving from what might be termed a 'super-model', is both the least misleading and the most fruitful for further discussion.[33]

Several times Ramsey emphasises the importance of being clear about the limitations of such traditional approaches, and now outdated phrases, to talk of God and evil.

'It is important that we realise what the logical pattern of such phrases is, and in particular we must *not* take them as belonging to the descriptive psychology of God. Rather are they once again, and like much philosophical theology and Christian doctrine, rules

93

for our consistent talking. They do not straightforwardly describe God. Rather do they tell us how we must talk about God if we wish to reckon squarely with the evil in the Universe, and at the same time to talk of him consistently, and always in reference to such empirical situations of "wonder" and "worship". . . .'[34]

The crucial point to note is that all such model-talk about God and evil, whether developed in terms of a multi-model pattern or a super-model pattern, must eventually, and for clarity's sake the sooner the better, be qualified more pointedly by the introduction of such qualifying terms as 'infinite', 'eternal', or 'supreme'.[35] Otherwise such models as 'permissive will' and 'purposive love' will be read as unqualified anthropomorphisms, thus failing to yield disclosures. In this way traditional Christian talk about God and evil can be seen to incorporate the basic model-qualifier pattern, and thus to make possible in principle both consistent talking and that disclosure of God in and through evil which any solution to the problem of evil requires.

Ramsey comes at the problem of evil from a different perspective in his response to Professor Mackie's article, 'Evil and Omnipotence'.[36] Mackie has claimed that the question of whether or not an omnipotent being can make something which he cannot control is a proper question which leads to a paradox. Ramsey replies that this question only leads to a paradox when the logic of 'omnipotent being' is assumed to be on the same logical level as 'human being' or 'knowledgeable being'. Since, according to Ramsey's interpretation, the logic of these two kinds of terms is not the same, he concludes that the question is an improper one.[37]

The logic of 'omnipotent' is, according to Ramsey, more like that of 'infinite sum' than it is like those terms which Mackie suggested. Here again the model-qualifier pattern can be seen to be operative. 'Potent' (or 'powerful') is a model which anchors the phrase in empirical experience. 'Omni-' (or 'all') is a qualifier which, far from simply suggesting anthropomorphic increase, serves to indicate a different logical pattern. The juxtaposition of these two terms builds a bridge from everyday experiences of power to a disclosure of that sort of power necessary to account for the existence of reality itself.[38]

This, then, is an account of the basic model-qualifier pattern which provides the framework for Ramsey's interpretation of Christian God-talk. The next section will focus on the way in which he understands the terminology of the Bible and theology from within the framework. In this connection, some attention will be given to Ramsey's account of the role of paradox in religion.

3 BIBLICAL AND THEOLOGICAL LANGUAGE[39]

With regard to the language of the Bible, Ramsey discusses a number of specific examples in some detail. However, since the primary focus of this present study is philosophical in nature, I shall limit my account to a brief survey of his findings. It should be noted that Ramsey finds biblical language more reflective of religious disclosure and commitment, while theological language, being more theoretical, is more reflective of the model-qualifier pattern.

In the Old Testament, Ramsey deals quite thoroughly with the process of developing names for God.[40] He traces the carefulness with which the Hebrews approached this difficult task, and sees in their refusal to pronounce the sacred Tetragrammaton an attempt to preserve the 'unseen' dimension of various disclosure-situations. Ramsey interprets the name-phrase 'I am because I am' as a significant tautology arising from a disclosure of the ultimacy of God in the same way that 'I must because I must' functions as a proper 'reason' in connection with moral obligation and 'I am I' brings an end to explanations of one's behaviour. Moreover, personal names themselves are often evocative of disclosures of personal knowledge.

> 'So far then, when it has been claimed that God has disclosed his name, what we have, in fact, is a characteristically religious situation with language appropriate to such a situation. Anything like a "name" escapes us. What is given in Ex. 3 as the name of God, is not a "name", as we would expect a name, but a phrase which is the best phrase man can use to talk of that full commitment in which his loyalty to God is expressed.'[41]

The Old Testament concept of prophecy is also seen by Ramsey as exhibiting the type of logic which is appropriate to disclosure-commitment situations.[42] He interprets the fulfilment of prophecy as having a twofold thrust: it applies to the spatio-temporal context of the prophet, and to the deeper religious dimension which is revealed by means of that context. Thus prophetic language both anchors itself in empirical experience, and qualifies that experience in such a way as to disclose a more profound dimension of experience. Isaiah's prophecy concerning the birth of a son is cited as an example of this twofold thrust of prophetic language.[43]

Turning to the New Testament, Ramsey analyses the ending of Mark's gospel and the account of Jesus' conversation with the Samaritan woman in order to bring out their disclosure-commitment structure.[44] He then discusses the Cross, the Resurrection, and the Ascension in some detail. In each case he stresses the fact that the event under consideration involves both a factual dimension and a religious dimension, neither of which is independent of the other.[45] The experiential relationship between these two dimensions was discussed in Chapter Three. The epistemological implications of this relationship will be taken up in detail in the next chapter.

Ramsey also takes up the topic of the various names and titles of Jesus. In *Religious Language*, he discusses the logical oddness of the phrase 'Son of Man' by way of indicating how it both describes and evokes a disclosure of the significance of who Jesus was, and how he related to the history of Israel.[46] Elsewhere, Ramsey considers a number of other titles of Jesus ranging from 'the Resurrection and the Life' to 'Messiah' and 'High Priest'. '. . . My contention [is] that the most significant titles of Jesus are those which incorporate and provide models which are grounded in a disclosure, on the one hand, and enable us to be reliably articulate about the Gospel, on the other.'[47]

With respect to theological language, Ramsey suggests that the history of Christian doctrine has been, and will continue to be, an ongoing attempt to systematise the language of the Bible and Christian experience. Models have been employed in order to ground doctrine in experience, and to make it intelligible. Qualifiers have been used in order to preserve the logical oddness of doctrinal language, and thus to ward off heresy. The use of both techniques can be seen in the development of the doctrines concerning the nature of Christ's relation to God the Father. 'Son' is used, for example, as a model, but is qualified by some such term as 'eternal' in order to preserve the experiential anchor and the logical uniqueness of the doctrine.

'As we survey the developments of Christology and Trinitarian doctrine, what is evident, however, is how often the heretics run some model or other—sometimes a highly sophisticated model— to death, in a passionate desire to understand. Opponents then come forward with other models which show the inadequacy of the first, but they too develop them beyond necessity, and court fresh heresies at the next move. . . . The shuttlecock character of the early history of Christian doctrine only arises because the ball could never be left to rest in any one empirical court. The struggle to understand God can never come to a satisfactory end; the language game can never be completed. Broadly speaking, what orthodoxy did was to support the winner of every heat.'[48]

Once again, Ramsey's major point about the language of Christian doctrine is that its logic is distinct from, but none the less related to, the language of descriptive science. However, he does venture to classify theological language into three broad categories for the purpose of offering some guide lines for understanding it. The Christian conviction that 'God did something through Jesus' may be developed in terms of the subject, namely God, and how He is to be thought of. Secondly, the Christian claim may be focused in terms of what was accomplished, namely redemption, by God's activity. Thirdly, the focus may be directed toward the objects, namely the Church and its worship (sacraments), resulting from God's activity.

In connection with developing the Christian conception of God, Ramsey says that 'what the early controversies settled were . . . rules for our talking, and what came out of them at the end were new symbols for our use, and in particular the Trinitarian formula'.[49] '. . . The creed is thus purely formal, and needs for its understanding and content the Christian disclosure. . . .'[50] In this way the doctrine of the Trinity is seen to exhibit the various models and qualifiers, in the terms 'Father', 'Son', and 'Holy Spirit', which are necessary to render God-talk appropriate to the full complexity of Christian religious experience.

Ramsey's handling of the locutions which attribute certain characteristics to God was discussed in an earlier section of this chapter. It should only be added that he gives the same sort of analysis, in terms of models and qualifiers, of the much-discussed phrase 'necessary being'.[51] He takes the term 'being' to function as a model and the term 'necessary' as a qualifier. Together they direct one to begin with particular beings and move to broader and broader conceptions of being whose existence is less and less contingent. Hopefully, an insight will dawn concerning the ultimacy of being itself, and the term 'God' is used to speak about what is thereby disclosed. In this way Ramsey suggests that the debate about the inappropriateness of attributing 'necessary' to an existent being can be seen to rest upon a confusion of logical categories.

Ramsey recommends the same sort of sensitivity when one considers the intricate logic of such terms as 'redemption', 'church', and 'sacrament'. An awareness of the double-dimension of religious terminology will enable one to avoid many of the mistakes which lead to an identification between 'redemption' and 'ethics', between 'church' and 'clergy' and between 'sacrament' and 'presence'. Although the former terms in each case are inextricably related to the latter terms, there is no simple, one-to-one correspondence between them.[52]

In yet another place, Ramsey gives a more thorough account of nearly the same Christian doctrines as he discusses in *Religious Language*. While with respect to the doctrines of the Church and of the sacraments he says much the same thing in both places, his account of the Trinity in 'A Logical Exploration of Some Christian Doctrines'[53] makes a further contribution. Herein he shows more precisely how the concept of the Trinity arose out of definite empirical experiences with Hebrew tradition, Jesus of Nazareth, the witness of the Apostles, and the convictions of the ongoing Church. When the various attempts to harmonise these strands are viewed as qualified models, many of the confusions of both theologians and anti-theologians can be absolved.

> 'What is quite plain is that the Trinity is not concerned to report on God's private life; it does not describe what goes on in the Godhead, it is no descriptive blueprint of God. The Doctrine of the Trinity is rather something which offers us complex logical guidance to talk about a mystery. We may say with Hilary that the doctrine is "helpful to man rather than . . . descriptive of God". It suggests rather than exhausts its theme.'[54]

One of the more popular and difficult notions lying at the heart of contemporary religious philosophy is that of paradox. I shall complete this examination of Ramsey's interpretation of theological language by delineating his understanding of this notion. The only place where he meets this issue head on is in his contribution to a symposium in a supplementary volume of the proceedings of the Aristotelian Society.[55] The other participant is Ninian Smart.

After granting that the notion of paradox is essential to religion, Ramsey asks, 'Can we do anything to distinguish illuminating and revealing improprieties from those which merely bewilder and confound us?'[56] He then proceeds to classify paradoxes according to the broad categories of 'avoidable' and 'unavoidable'. Within each of these broad categories Ramsey suggests two subdivisions, and then sets himself to an analysis of each of them.

Among avoidable paradoxes Ramsey discusses those which are 'retrospectively negative' in their results, and those which are 'subsequently significant'. The former are paradoxes that are seen, upon analysis, to be examples of what Ryle calls 'category mistakes'. That is, they are based on a confusing interrelating of language levels which are logically distinct. Ramsey suggests that attempts to expound the doctrine of the Trinity in terms of physical models alone are examples of this type of negative, and avoidable, paradox.

Other avoidable paradoxes are those that can, at a later date, be worked through, or overcome. These prove their worth by bringing together two aspects of experience that at the outset seem to conflict with one another, and thereby forcing the thinkers involved to develop a more encompassing model. They are avoidable if and when they are subsequently significant. Ramsey mentions the 'wave/particle paradox' which is presently confounding and spurring theoretic physicists, as a possible example. In the theological realm he points to the paradox of the divine/human nature of Christ as a possible example of a subsequently significant, and thus avoidable, paradox. Ramsey's concern to go 'beyond paradox' clearly distinguishes him from those religious thinkers who prefer to 'wallow' in it.

Among unavoidable paradoxes Ramsey delineates those which are 'logically inaccessible' and those which are 'logically explorable'. About the former he contends there is nothing to say. Silence is the only appropriate response. He seems to imply that it is no less, and perhaps even more, religious to refuse to talk about such paradoxes than it is to profess to 'accept' them by a 'leap' of faith. It is this type of paradox which Ramsey seems to equate with logical incoherence. The logically explorable paradoxes are those which can be made sense of when viewed in terms of Ramsey's model-qualifier schema. He contends that often the terms of an unavoidable paradox can be shown to exhibit the characteristics of model-terms and qualifier-terms, respectively. When certain key terms are seen to function as, and here Ramsey uses Willard V. O. Quine's term, 'irreducible posits',[57] the paradox which they generate in juxtaposition with empirical terms is seen as logically odd, but not as logically inaccessible.[58] The operation of such qualifier-terms in theology differs very little from their operation in mathematics and logic.

Ramsey is aware of the position in which his interpretation of paradox places him with respect to existentialist thinkers. He specifically mentions Kierkegaard and Karl Barth, although his actual criticisms are directed more toward the latter than the former.[59] Ramsey agrees wholeheartedly with such kerygmatic thinkers that the response of commitment is absolutely essential to the religious situation. Moreover, he is also in agreement that religious and theological language is not to be understood as some sort of 'super-science'. However, Ramsey disagrees with Barth and others who maintain that no account whatsoever can be given of the basis and nature of religious discernment and commitment. Furthermore, Ramsey finds Barth guilty of projecting the logical oddness of the term 'God' to God Himself. Thus his one-sided concern with God's 'otherness' betrays a reliance upon a theory of language which assumes a one-to-one representational correspondence between words and things. Finally, Ramsey criticises Barth for confusing the certainty of religious experience with that of theological assertions. The distinction which Ramsey draws between these two forms of certainty will be discussed more fully in the next chapter.

Turning his focus to the consideration of paradoxes which involve the term 'God', Ramsey begins by agreeing with Kierkegaard and other existentialists who insist on the basic importance and uniqueness of knowledge and language about oneself. Although there are points of difference, Ramsey is impressed with Kierkegaard's concern to stress the logical and experiential primacy of self-awareness. Moreover, Kierkegaard's emphasis on the mediational function of self-awareness in bringing about a disclosure of religious awareness is in harmony with Ramsey's emphasis on the importance of the logic of 'I' for mapping the logic of 'God'. So it is that Ramsey suggests that 'God paradoxes' must be understood as essentially similar to those paradoxes arising from the attempt to be articulate about self-awareness.[60] Both 'God' and 'I' arise in response to a disclosure which goes beyond, but is based in, factual experience.

Ramsey concludes by warning against two opposite, but equally irreligious, attitudes toward religious paradox. The one is to deny the place of paradox in religion by interpreting religious language as object-talk. Both religious and non-religious people have been guilty of this attitude. The other is to refuse to explore the logic of religious language by interpreting it as being entirely beyond comprehension. Here too, both religious and non-religious people have been guilty.

100

Ramsey summarises his analysis in the following way:

'What I have tried to allow for is genuine mystery in the sense that "what there is" is not restricted to observables, and to suggest that it is as apt currency for such mystery that there arises "mysterious paradox", which is then neither a vicious muddle nor an inaccessible incantation, but paradox whose structure can be investigated and explored under the guidance of the logical behaviour of "I".'[61]

4 'GOD' AS AN INTEGRATOR TERM

In addition to his interpretation of God-talk in terms of the model-qualifier pattern, Ramsey also develops an interpretation of the more theoretic function of the term 'God' itself. As will become clear shortly, this interpretation does not conflict with, but rather complements, his earlier treatment. The following discussion of this additional function of the term 'God' will complete this chapter on Ramsey's understanding of the nature of Christian God-talk.

In attempting to make a case for the construction of a metaphysics that is both cognitively meaningful and worthy of its name, Ramsey lays the groundwork for an understanding of the theoretic function of the term 'God'. He sees the broad purpose of all theoretic language as integrative in nature. That is, theoretic language is introduced and related to ordinary language in order to integrate the divergencies which occur in connection with the latter. In terms of a map-making analogy, Ramsey sees theoretic language as an attempt to construct a large-scale map which encompasses and unifies a number of small-scale maps.[62]

The theoretic languages of mathematics, logic, and physics are discussed briefly as examples of large-scale, integrating maps. The language of mathematics is interpreted by Ramsey as a theoretic construct which enables one to generalise about such widely diverse entities as five cows and five fingers, and the relation between the radii and circumferences of various spherical objects. 'Mathematics in this way provides languages such as arithmetic, algebraical geometry and trigonometrical analysis, which, brought alongside common-sense language, can help to unite what is apparently diverse, can help us to attain wide sweeps of generalisation.'[63]

Relying on the insights of P. F. Strawson,[64] Ramsey contends that the language-game of logic fulfils a similar function as mathematics in relationship to ordinary language. Although the more generalised

101

a logical system becomes, the less it resembles ordinary language, it must always maintain an essential connection at certain key points in order to be of use. Logical language thus serves an integrative function in relationship to the various statements of ordinary language, in that it unifies it into a coherent system of expression and argumentation.

Ramsey interprets the language of theoretic physics in much the same way, calling attention to its generalising purpose. The whole point of developing laws and hypotheses about the behaviour of physical objects is to be able to unify vastly diverse phenomena into one, large-scale language schema. By bringing the language of physics alongside of ordinary statements about specific phenomena, one is able to integrate one's understanding and talk about those phenomena with one's understanding and talk about other phenomena. Using the old problem of the straight stick which looks bent when half submerged in water, Ramsey suggests that the language of physics, in terms of 'refraction', enables us to unite 'The stick is bent' and 'The stick is straight'.[65]

Turning to the language of metaphysics, Ramsey maintains that it too is to be understood as a theoretic schema which aims at constructing a large-scale language map encompassing the many small-scale maps of ordinary language. Thus he suggests that rather than interpreting the metaphysical debate concerning 'appearance' and 'reality' as an exercise in 'superscience', one ought to interpret it as the introduction of a

'. . . large-scale map by which to illuminate and organise the diverse assertions of ordinary language. For instance when a metaphysician says "Evil is really only good misperceived", he need not deny any common-sense talk about good and evil. He certainly need not deny that for us all there is a perfectly proper use of the word "evil". At the same time, by his metaphysical assertion he is expressing his option for some map which while allowing all that, believes talk about good and evil to be most reliably structured, and its logical relations best shown, by a large-scale map which includes no talk about evil at all.'[66]

In this way, according to Ramsey, metaphysics can be seen to take its place alongside the other theoretic language-games. It is neither simply an extension of, nor a replacing of, ordinary language. Although it overlaps with the latter at certain crucial points, its logic is on another level altogether. Such a view of metaphysics side-steps many of the criticisms directed at the traditional view.[67]

On the other hand, it must not be thought that the language of metaphysics can be entirely assimilated to the languages of the theoretic sciences. There is an important difference between them as well. The difference arises from the fact that the languages of the various sciences cannot be integrated, or united, apart from a yet broader language map which encompasses them, but goes beyond them as well. Ramsey thinks that metaphysics can be interpreted as seeking to provide such a language map. This type of metaphysics must be based upon a logic which both enables it to be somewhat unique and to be empirically controlled.

'The consequent cost of a total overall map, of the kind the metaphysicians seek, is integrator words not native to any of the diverse observational languages of the sciences, yet able to combine with and supplement them: words which, while able in this way to secure a reference to observables by associating with scientific discourse, are not confined within its logical patterns.'[68]

Ramsey concludes that this type of metaphysics is only possible if terms can be found which not only unite the various language-maps of ordinary language and theoretic science, but which also have as their basis a disclosure of a dimension of experience which goes beyond the totality of observables. Here again it is important to note that Ramsey is not opting for some 'ghosty' world beyond observable experience, but rather for a dimension of experience that is mediated in and through observables, which is none the less real for not being reducible to them. At this point he returns to what proves to be the cornerstone of his entire position; namely, to the unique logic of knowledge and talk about the self. '. . . the situation which justifies metaphysics is very like what justifies for each of us our own use of "I", and that in this word "I" we have a paradigm for all metaphysical integrators'.[69] Since the logic of 'I' has been discussed in detail already, no attempt will be made to retrace Ramsey's analysis.

On the basis of this understanding of metaphysical language, Ramsey suggests that 'God' be explored as an integrator term offered by the metaphysical language map known as 'Theism'.[70] He believes 'God' 'to be the integrator word which provides the most simple, far-reaching and coherent metaphysical map'.[71] The first step of such an exploration of the term 'God' is to model it on the term 'I'. God-talk, like I-talk, obtains currency as the most

103

appropriate way to speak about the dimension of reality which is discerned in certain disclosure-situations.

> 'The possibility of a metaphysical theology arises when, to talk of the objective constituent of all disclosure situations which go beyond what is seen, to unite the various metaphysical words that are cast up in this way, we use the word "God". This word "God" is modelled on, though it has necessarily important differences from, "I". These differences are in fact grounded in the observable features of those various disclosure situations which more aptly lead us to God rather than to ourselves or other people.'[72]

God-talk is thus every bit as philosophically respectable as is I-talk. Both function as metaphysical integrator terms which both unite other forms and levels of discourse, and call attention to aspects of experience that transcend the spatio-temporal environment.

In another context, Ramsey draws certain parallels between models used for God and the use of models in the theoretic sciences.[73] He first distinguishes between 'picture' models and 'analogue' models. The former are devised in order to establish a one-to-one correspondence between their own elements and those of the aspect of reality they are expected to model. The latter are set up in order to establish a functional, or structural, relationship between themselves and the aspect of reality being studied. Models for God clearly fall into this latter classification. The criterion for evaluating such a model is its fruitfulness in enabling one to be helpfully, but not exhaustively, articulate about any given dimension of experience. This question of evaluation will be taken up in detail in the next chapter.

It is in this way, then, that God-talk is understood by Ramsey. It arises in response to a disclosure-commitment situation, and is thus no more 'odd' than I-talk, or the language of theoretical science. Its essential pattern is that of models and qualifiers, and this pattern is clearly seen in biblical and theological discourse. Finally, God-talk is also seen as fulfilling an integrative purpose in relationship to ordinary and scientific language, to the degree that it functions as a 'chastened metaphysical' term.

> 'Christian doctrine does not give a picture of God in the sense of a verbal photograph. Christian doctrine can only be justified on

an epistemology very different from that which lay behind traditional views of metaphysics. In no sense is Christian doctrine a
"superscience". Its structure, and its anchorage in "fact" are
much more complex than that parallel would suggest. What we
have been trying to do in these various examples has been to
give hints—no more—of how traditional Christian phrases might
otherwise be elucidated and justified. If they are anchored in
"disclosure" situations, situations which centre directly or in-
directly on Jesus of Nazareth and are in part mysterious and
elusive, only then can Christian phrases be given a logical complexity suited to their theme.'[74]

NOTES

1 *Freedom and Immortality*, p. 152.
2 *Religious Language*, pp. 55–6.
3 Cf. Ludwig Wittgenstein, *Philosophical Investigations*, Part 1, para-
   graphs nos. 404–14, and Part 2, Section no. 10; Gilbert Ryle, *The
   Concept of Mind*, pp. 191ff.; P. F. Strawson, 'Persons', *Individuals*.
4 *Religious Language*, p. 54.
5 Ian Ramsey, 'The Systematic Elusiveness of "I" ', *Philosophical
   Quarterly*, V, no. 20 (July 1955), p. 193; *Christian Empiricism*, pp. 17–31.
   Also *Religion and Science: Conflict and Synthesis*, pp. 26–48.
6 David Hume, *A Treatise of Human Nature*, Book 1, Part 4, Section
   6, and Appendix.
7 Ramsey, 'Biology and Personality', *Philosophical Forum*, XXI (1964),
   pp. 36–7. Also in *Christian Empiricism*, pp. 42–3.
8 Ryle, *Concept of Mind*, pp. 191ff.
9 'The Systematic Elusiveness of "I" ', p. 196; *Christian Empiricism*, p. 22.
10 ibid., p. 197; *Christian Empiricism*, p. 22.
11 ibid., p. 197; *Christian Empiricism*, p. 22.
12 ibid., pp. 198ff; *Christian Empiricism*, pp. 23ff.
13 ibid., pp. 201–2; *Christian Empiricism*, pp. 27–9.
14 ibid., pp. 202–3; *Christian Empiricism*, pp. 29–30.
15 ibid., pp. 203–4; *Christian Empiricism*, pp. 30–1.
16 *Religious Language*, p. 69.
17 ibid., p. 70.
18 ibid., p. 77.
19 'On Understanding Mystery', *Chicago Theological Seminary Register*,
   LIII, no. 5 (May 1963), pp. 11–12. Also in *Christian Empiricism*, p. 74.
20 *Religious Language*, pp. 57ff.
21 ibid., p. 57.
22 ibid., pp. 60ff.
23 ibid., p. 67.
24 ibid., pp. 69ff.
25 ibid., p. 69.
26 ibid., pp. 70, 76.
27 ibid., p. 79.

28 *Religious Language*, pp. 85–9.
29 'On Understanding Mystery', pp. 9–10. Also in *Christian Empiricism*, pp. 70–1.
30 ibid., p. 10. Also in *Christian Empiricism*, p. 72.
31 'Philosophy of Religion' (unpublished notes), pp. 20–6.
32 *Religious Language*, pp. 92–100.
33 ibid., p. 99, and 'Philosophy of Religion' (unpublished notes), p. 25.
34 ibid., p. 96.
35 This same point is made with regard to 'Atonement Theology' in *Christian Discourse*, pp. 28–60.
36 J. L. Mackie, 'Evil and Omnipotence', *Mind*, LXIV, no. 254 (April 1955), pp. 200ff.
37 Ramsey, 'The Paradox of Omnipotence', *Mind*, LXV, no. 258 (April 1956), p. 263.
38 ibid., pp. 265ff.
39 Although most of the following section will be based upon an analysis of *Religious Language*, what Ramsey says there is amply supplemented by his *Christian Discourse: Some Logical Explorations*.
40 *Religious Language*, pp. 124–9.
41 ibid., p. 128.
42 ibid., pp. 130–40.
43 ibid., p. 137.
44 ibid., pp. 141–5.
45 ibid., pp. 145–59.
46 ibid., pp. 159–67.
47 Ramsey, 'On Being Articulate About the Gospel', *Chicago Theological Seminary Register*, LIII, no. 5 (May 1963), p. 13. Cf. *Christian Empiricism*, p. 77.
48 *Religious Language*, pp. 197–8.
49 ibid., p. 202.
50 ibid., p. 208.
51 'On Understanding Mystery', pp. 7–9. Also in *Christian Empiricism*, pp. 67–8.
52 *Religious Language*, pp. 208–14.
53 Ramsey, 'A Logical Exploration of Some Christian Doctrines', *Chicago Theological Seminary Register*, LIII, no. 5 (May 1963), p. 26.
54 ibid., p. 38.
55 Ramsey, 'Paradox in Religion', *Proceedings of The Aristotelian Society*, Supplementary Vol. XXXIII (1959), p. 195. Also in *Christian Empiricism*, pp. 98–119.
56 ibid., p. 195; *Christian Empiricism*, p. 98.
57 W. V. O. Quine, *From a Logical Point of View*, p. 44.
58 'Paradox in Religion', p. 208. Also in *Christian Empiricism*, p. 110.
59 ibid., pp. 210ff; *Christian Empiricism*, pp. 112ff.
60 ibid., p. 215; *Christian Empiricism*, p. 116.
61 ibid., p. 218; *Christian Empiricism*, p. 118.
62 *Prospect for Metaphysics*, pp. 153ff.
63 ibid., p. 155.
64 P. F. Strawson, *Introduction to Logical Theory*, pp. 57–8.
65 *Prospect for Metaphysics*, p. 157.
66 ibid., p. 158.

67   ibid., pp. 159–60.
68   ibid., p. 161.
69   ibid., pp. 163ff.
70   This suggestion is also developed in connection with 'the honest-to-God-debate' on pages 61–90 of Ramsey's *Christian Discourse*.
71   *Prospect for Metaphysics*, p. 164.
72   ibid., p. 174.
73   Ramsey, *Models and Mystery*, Chapter 1.
74   *Religious Language*, p. 198.

Chapter 5

THE CONFIRMATION OF RELIGIOUS KNOWLEDGE

It is helpful to think of Ramsey's overall position as forming what might be called an 'epistemological arc'. That is to say, there is an implicit logical structure to his position which expresses itself in the movement from experience to language and back to experience again. It is in this sense that Ramsey is to be classified as an empiricist.

I have endeavoured to make this implicit structure explicit in the development of this study. After beginning with an account of the sort of experiential situation which gives rise to religious insight and commitment, I turned to a discussion of the type of language that is employed in connection with these situations and commitments. But no empiricist epistemology is satisfactory until the arc has been completed by returning once again to experience. The question of the criteria for distinguishing between truth and error is absolutely crucial to philosophy in general, and to the problem of religious language in particular. Thus it is time to turn to a discussion of Ramsey's views concerning the verification, or confirmation, of Christian language.

This final chapter in my presentation of Ramsey's position will begin with an account of his understanding of the relation between science and religion, and then will move to a discussion of his interpretation of religious confirmation. It will conclude with a consideration of the implications of this view with respect to the nature of Christian knowledge.

1 SCIENCE AND RELIGION

Because of his background in the sciences, Ramsey is especially anxious, and qualified, to discuss the relationship between science and religion. Furthermore, such a discussion is especially crucial in light of the fact that the original challenge of logical empiricism was posed in terms of the relationship between the two fields. Indeed, the question of the nature of religious confirmation would seem to depend upon the way in which one interprets this relationship.

As would be expected, Ramsey takes a position on this question which seeks to avoid two equally dangerous, but highly popular, extremes.[1] On the one hand, he is careful to avoid the view which identifies the concerns of science and religion. This view not only fails to understand the personal and transcendent nature of religion, but it inevitably leads to a conflict between science and religion which the latter is bound to lose as the former continues to develop. This is a view which both religious and non-religious people have taken.

'So we conclude this first reflection by denying that the language of science could ever expand so as to deal with all that religious language talks about. For religious language is grounded in the personal, and we have now seen that the personal is not only a category which is never wholly reducible to scientific terms, but that (more positively) it interlocks with all the diverse languages of science to unite them as a common presupposition.[2]

On the other hand, Ramsey is equally eager to avoid the view which maintains an absolute dichotomy between the concerns of religion and science. This view, which is especially popular on the contemporary scene among the religious and non-religious alike, is actually in harmony with the conclusion of the argument offered by logical empiricism. Such a view confuses logical diversity with absolute autonomy, and thus fails to grasp the experiential basis and unifying nature of religious discourse. 'More positively, it is precisely because the word "God" has its own peculiar logical behaviour, a behaviour only approached by the word "I", that the languages of science can be significantly united by assertions incorporating the word of "God". . . .'[3]

Ramsey endeavours to point out the similarities and differences between science and religion, in order to explicate the nature of the relationship between them, by tracing the main stages of the scientific method. In his view, this method begins with numerous individual assertions about various observable aspects of experience.

However, until simple generalisations are made on the basis of these individual observational assertions, the scientific method is not really functioning. It is important to be aware of the fact that, although these observations can be said to give rise to these generalisations, in no sense are the latter deduced from the former. Upon being confronted with a variety of empirical facts and/or assertions, a scientist may discern a pattern which leads him to make a generalisation. Thus the generalisation, while being impossible apart from the observations, clearly goes beyond them. In Ramsey's terminology, the observables give rise to a 'disclosure' which includes them and transcends them at the same time. The disclosed generalisation is mediated by means of the observables.[4]

The similarities between science and religion on this initial experiential level are obvious. The main difference is in the contrast between the subject matter of the two endeavours. Science concerns itself with physical behaviour which can be described in object language, while religion is concerned with personal and moral experience which cannot be so described.

The next main stage of scientific procedure is the transformation of the original, simple generalisations into large-scale hypotheses on the basis of modifications resulting from additional data. Here, too, the element of disclosure plays an important part in providing the insight enabling the scientist to conceive the large-scale hypothesis. Such an insight may be expressed in mathematical or metaphysical terms, or both. The exact language of mathematics is, of course, used widely as is the case when a mathematical point is designated as x, y, or z. However, it is very often supplemented at crucial points with the use of such non-literal terms as 'particle', 'force', and 'mass'. In a word, the language of science, when it becomes sufficiently complex to produce highly useful theories, must employ model-terms which serve to unify and regulate the observational terms. Ramsey contends that even 'operationalism' falls back on such irreducible and indefinable posits.[5]

Here again the parallels between science and religion on this theoretic and linguistic level are quite clear. Both employ and combine language from the observational level (model-terms) and from the more-than-observational level (qualifier-terms). Once again, the primary difference between them is their point of focus. Science focuses on physical phenomena while religion focuses on personal experience.

The final stage of scientific endeavour, according to Ramsey, is the constant, but never-ending, attempt to unify the language of science by converting the various large-scale hypotheses into one large-scale map, or theory. As was pointed out in the last section of Chapter Four, Ramsey is convinced that this stage in scientific procedure, while fruitful in the development of more encompassing hypotheses, can never be completed apart from the introduction of metaphysical and/or religious terminology. He contends that the desire to construct an all-encompassing and unifying language map cannot be fulfilled within the framework of science alone because that framework systematically eliminates all terms that relate to the personal dimension of experience. Moreover, science itself, in using one theory, necessarily excludes others and thereby limits itself. Since any language map which is going to unify all language levels and fields must necessarily encompass talk about personal experience as well, it follows that the language of science stands in need of being supplemented by the language of metaphysics and/or religion.[6]

Once again it should be stressed that Ramsey is not opting for a return to a metaphysical language which traffics in 'word-magic' willy-nilly. On the contrary, he is opting for the employment of key terms and concepts which, while anchored in empirical experience, serve to integrate the various levels and fields of language. Certain crucial terms, such as 'I' and 'God', must be, and in ordinary language always have been, employed to do justice to the facts of human experience. Thus Ramsey concludes that the languages of science and religion, while being logically distinct, can and must be related in a functional manner.[7]

In spite of the similarities between science and religion on such matters as their basis in experiential disclosure and their employment of key, non-empirical terms, there is a difference between them when it comes to the question of verification. Although he maintains that it is possible to confirm religious utterances, Ramsey is careful to point out that the form of confirmation appropriate to religion is far more similar to that involved in personal knowledge than it is to that employed by the physical sciences.

The exact nature of religious confirmation will be taken up in the next section. Suffice it to say at this point that the major difference between it and scientific confirmation, in Ramsey's view, pertains to the question of deductive predictions.[8] The terms and concepts employed in science can be controlled in such a way as to yield deductive predictions about future experience. Such predictions render the procedure of confirmation exceedingly precise. The terms and concepts employed in personal and religious experience, however, cannot be so controlled, and consequently do not yield strict predictions. Thus the confirmation of religious assertions is a much less precise, but none the less adequate, procedure. This essential difference between the key terms of science and religion stems, as has already been mentioned, from the fact that their logical functions are distinct. The key terms of science, such as 'particle' and 'mass', function as a conceptual bridge between empirical observations and experimental verification. For this reason, they can be operationally connected to empirical predictions. The key terms of religion, however, like those of 'chastened' metaphysics, function as integrators and unifiers in relationship to the languages of the sciences, by way of providing an overall language map. For this reason they do not logically entail any empirical predictions. In this way the term 'God' functions very much like the term 'I'. The use of both is ultimately entailed by all empirical assertions, while neither entails any specific empirical assertions.

'We thus have the vision of a compact language map wherein all the diverse languages of science are harmonised, without confounding type differences, and without committing category blunders. It is a map on which assertions incorporating the word "God"—of whose logical behaviour "I" provides some kind of reflection—occupy a central, presiding position, being entailed by, but themselves entailing none of these assertions of natural science; and the whole map is anchored in, and finds its empirical basis in a cosmic disclosure, when we respond to what is disclosed, and what is mediated to us, through the patterns of the natural world.'[9]

Before going on, it might prove helpful to sketch the implications for religion which Ramsey thinks follow from the foregoing account of the relation between it and science. It is at this point that the empiricist thrust of Ramsey's position becomes especially clear. As has been stressed throughout this study, Ramsey adamantly insists upon the experiential basis of religion in terms of disclosure situations. Religious insight and commitment do not occur as the result of deductive arguments, nor in some sort of 'fiedeistic vacuum'. On Ramsey's view, God reveals Himself by means of human experience.

Going yet further in the empiricist tradition, Ramsey also stresses the importance of constantly testing and evaluating the concepts and assertions of one's religion. Religious language, especially Christian God-talk, must always be scrutinised and explored so as to

112

keep it from becoming cognitively misleading and experientially irrelevant. Such a procedure will inevitably lead to continual revision and qualification. Ramsey views this result as an asset, rather than as a liability. 'Science and religion may find a synthesis in their methods. But the cost to each is great. The theologian must admit a tentative theology; the scientist must admit key words which cannot (and it is a logical *cannot*) be given straight scientific verification.'[10]

2 EMPIRICAL FIT

Against the background of the foregoing discussion of Ramsey's interpretation of the relation between science and religion, I shall now turn to a consideration of his view of religious confirmation. His overall argument moves from an analysis of the nature and verification of scientific models to an examination of theological models, and finally to the conclusion that the latter are open to confirmation in much the same way as the former. Obviously, the validity of Ramsey's argument depends upon the accuracy of his analysis of both kinds of models. His most thorough treatment of this topic is found in his *Models and Mystery*, and this book will provide the basis for the following discussion.

The cornerstone upon which Ramsey's understanding of models is based is the distinction between 'picture' models and 'analogue' models. For this distinction, as well as for several other major points, Ramsey acknowledges his indebtedness to Max Black's *Models and Metaphors*.[11] The core of the distinction lies in the fact that picturing, or 'scale', models seek to reproduce the various features of that aspect of experience which they are modelling, while analogue, or 'functional', models seek to display the structure of the reality under consideration. Classical physics made almost exclusive use of the former, while contemporary physics makes increasing use of the latter. Ramsey laments the fact that traditionally the language of theology has been interpreted strictly in terms of picture models.[12]

Although picture models, whether in science or theology, have the distinct advantage of enabling one to speak significantly about definite characteristics of reality, they also have serious disadvantages.[13] One such disadvantage is the tendency toward distortion and conflict whenever the scope of such models is expanded beyond the original purpose. Another disadvantage is that an exclusive reliance upon this type of model automatically eliminates the elements of transcendence and mystery. Thus it is that picture models stand in need of complementation by analogue models. On the basis of this distinction, Ramsey makes the point that the more reliable and fruitful theological models are those of the analogue variety.[14] As has been seen, this same point, although in somewhat different terminology, is used often by Ramsey.

After reiterating the positive functions of model-talk in theology, Ramsey 'zeros in' on the specific problem of confirmation. He contends that scientific analogue models are, and must be, evaluated according to a twofold criterion. First, 'structurally the model must somehow or other chime in with and echo the phenomena'.[15] In other words, the model must correspond to, or cohere with, that dimension of reality which originally gave rise to the model. Second, in science 'a model is the better the more prolific it is in generating deductions which are then open to experimental verification and falsification'.[16] That model which is both widely testable and confirmable is superior to, or more 'true' than, those which are not.

Turning again to the confirmation of theological models, Ramsey once again insists that there are both similarities and differences between them and those of science. As in science, the models of theology must be consistent with, and appropriate to, the experiential disclosure to which they relate, whether they have generated the disclosure, or arisen with it.

'There must be something about the universe and man's experience in it which, for example, matches the behaviour of a loving father. . . . In other words, there are on the one hand certain situations in which we find ourselves, certain situations of a cosmic character, which in virtue of some feature or other echo, chime in with, are isomorphous with other situations in which we speak, for example, of strong towers, of kingship, of fathers and sons, and the two together, because of the common feature, generate insight.'[17]

Here then, in the nature of their experiential source, the models of theology and science are essentially the same. Without this experiential basis no model can function adequately as a language map.

Unlike the models of science, however, the models of theology can never provide specific predictions which will serve to confirm or disconfirm it in an experimental fashion. 'A model in theology does not stand or fall with, a theological model is not judged for its success or failure by reference to, the possibility of verifiable deductions.'[18] There are two reasons which Ramsey gives for this crucial difference. First, as has been stressed earlier in this study, high-level theological models, such as those for God, have a distinct logic. That is, their purpose is not to provide a conceptual bridge between initial and verifiable observations, but is rather to provide an overall language map which will serve to integrate the many other language maps. Second, the models of theology are patterned after those of personal experience and discourse, rather than those of physical experience. Such a pattern necessarily renders their logic much more complex and systematically elusive than those of the sciences. The distinct logic and personal nature of theological models thus eliminate the possibility of deducing specific predictions from them.

All of this is not to say, however, that Ramsey thinks theological models are immune to any form of confirmation. On the contrary, he is especially concerned to maintain both the possibility and the necessity of their confirmation and/or disconfirmation. A theological model is not evaluated by its ability to fulfil predictions. 'It is rather judged by its stability over the widest possible range of phenomena, by its ability to incorporate the most diverse phenomena not inconsistently. . . . As a model in theology is developed, it rather stands or falls according to its success (or otherwise) in harmonising whatever events are to hand.'[19]

Ramsey conceives of the sort of confirmation which is appropriate to religious language, and/or theological models, as more akin to the sort operative within inter-personal relationships. Although not nearly as precise as the confirmation achieved in the sciences, this form is clearly adequate, and may even prove to be more comprehensive in the long run. He terms this sort of confirmation 'empirical fit', and describes it in the following fashion:

'The theological model works more like the fitting of a boot or a shoe than like the "yes" or "no" of a roll call. In other words, we have a particular doctrine which, like a preferred and selected shoe, starts by appearing to meet our empirical needs. But on closer fitting to the phenomena the shoe may pinch. When tested against future slush and rain it may be proven to be not altogether watertight or it may be comfortable—yet it must not be too comfortable. In this way, the test of a shoe is measured by its ability to match a wide range of phenomena, by its overall success in meeting a variety of needs. Here is what I might call the method of empirical fit which is displayed by theological theorising. . . . It is significantly different from the verifiable deductions of scientific theorising, and it is undoubtedly important to see where, in ways like this, models in science differ from models in theology. But, for our overall purpose, it is even more important to see where they resemble each other and, most important of all, to see where they face the same problem and may each embrace the same solution.'[20]

Further on in his book Ramsey returns to the concept of empirical fit in connection with a discussion of the models that are operative in psychology and the social sciences. After stressing the necessity of models based on a personal pattern, and after reiterating the uniqueness of persons and personal knowledge, he again sets forth the main characteristics of his key epistemological concept. Theology, like psychology and the social sciences, must employ personal models.

'These will be the models whose links with observable facts are not predictive, after the fashion of scientific models. These models will work in terms of what in the first lecture I called empirical fit. For it is empirical fit, rather than deductive verifications, which characterises models which are distinctively personal. Let me illustrate. From "*a* loves *b*" nothing can be rigorously deduced which permits of appeal to experiment and consequent verification or falsification. For instance, someone might allege that if "*a* loves *b*" there will be some occasion when *a* will be found planning for *b*'s happiness; but *a* might some day plan for *b*'s happiness simply in the hope of favours to come—and apparent experimental verification would be wholly deceptive. Alternatively, from "*a* loves *b*" someone might suppose that *a* would never be seen for example in any sort of way which might cause *b* even momentary unhappiness. But this would be a far too shallow view of human relationships; love indeed is "deepened", through tensions lived through and redeemed. In brief, "*a* loves *b*" will only be verified in terms of what I called in the last lecture "empirical fit" and the test will be how stable the assertion is as an overall characterisation of a complex, multivaried pattern of behaviour which it is impossible in a particular case to specify deductively beforehand.'[21]

Here is the core of Ramsey's understanding of religious confirmation! The experiential pattern is that of personal knowledge, the test is that of a broadly conceived coherence, and the resultant knowledge is adequate, but far more personal and tentative than many theologians would care to admit. The specific nature of this knowledge will be discussed in the next section. The main point of Ramsey's position is that the choice between strict scientific verification and subjective relativity does not exhaust the alternatives. He is opting for a view of confirmation which is appropriate in such matters as personal and religious experience, and which is none the less adequate for being less precise. In fact, the implicit assumption of Ramsey's explicit arguments is that such a conception of confirmation is already operative in, to borrow a phrase from John Wild, 'the world of ordinary language'.[22]

It is on this ground that Ramsey faces the question concerning the reality of the referents of religious language and theological models. He contends that, often, contemporary physicists and philosophers of science, to say nothing of theologians, have failed to follow through on the implications of the modern view of models. Although they reject the exclusive use of picturing models, they refuse to assign any ontological status to the model referents, thus continuing to view the models as only intellectual constructs. Ramsey, on the other hand, takes a more radical, and he thinks more consistent, view when he follows the insights of such thinkers as Max Black and W. V. O. Quine.[23]

'But now we must emphasise that models in science not only enable us to generate verifiable deductions, and models in theology not only make possible empirical fit. They each arise out of, and in this way become currency for, a universe that discloses itself to us in a moment of insight. The disclosure which accompanies the birth of a model reveals to us what scientific models and theological models contrive in their various ways to understand.'[24]

This ontological commitment is based on the 'pragmatic', to use Quine's term, rule of thumb which grants ontological status to whatever establishes itself as an essential and necessary component of a given language map. The reality of the referents of such concepts as class-terms and 'God' is no less 'real' for being logically different from the referents of physical object terms. The language of theology, including and especially the term 'God', has been developed to enable a very large number of people to speak about a dimension of reality which reveals itself in disclosure-situations.

Such language may be discredited by means of standards appropriate to it, but should not be elminated as meaningless *a priori*.[25] 'Certainly it is from ordinary language that precision language takes its rise, and we must not be so dazzled by the precision polish that we neglect the rock whence it was hewn.'[26]

With regard to the confirmation of specifically Christian language and experience, the category of history becomes especially significant. This is particularly the case within contemporary theology, where a heated debate rages over the role of history in the Christian religion. Ramsey addresses himself to this question in an essay entitled 'History and the Gospels: Some Philosophical Reflections'.[27] It will be both appropriate and profitable to give an analysis of his account of the relationship between history and religious confirmation.

Ramsey begins by sketching the two dominant, but somewhat extreme, positions on the theological market. On one side stand those who have maintained that for the understanding and confirmation of Christianity the 'plain hard facts' are what really matter. This view, often most closely associated with traditional orthodoxy, interprets revelation as informational in nature, and faith as a form of mental assent. On the other side stand those who have maintained that Christian faith has nothing whatsoever to do with the 'plain hard facts' of history. This view, strangely enough, often brings together proponents of both existentialism and logical empiricism. Here revelation, when allowed, is understood as having to do with the quality of one's life, rather than with information, and faith is interpreted as a commitment to Christ's way of life.

It is in connection with this issue that the concerns of both contemporary theology and philosophy are brought together. The 'Jesus of history versus the Christ of faith' debate blends into the conflict of responses to the challenge of logical empiricism as outlined in Part One. Ramsey's concern is to mediate between these extreme positions and issues in order to salvage the insights and avoid the shortcomings of each.[28] He rejects the extreme positions of conservatism, whether philosophical or theological, on the one hand, and the existentialism of Bultmann and Tillich on the other.[29]

The two points which provide the key to what Ramsey takes to be a more adequate view are similar to those which have been discussed in the first part of this section. The first point pertains to the modern understanding of history which sees the necessity of defining history as in some way involving 'facts plus interpretation'.[30] It is now commonly acknowledged that there are no such things as the 'plain hard facts' of history. The strictures of selectivity, contextualism, and perspective eliminate such a possibility. The second point pertains to the fact that models employed in historical language and theory are necessarily personal in nature. This fact renders the language of history a more appropriate vehicle for the expression of the religious dimension than the language of science. Both of these points make apparent the need for the language map of history to be supplemented by a broader, more philosophical language map which is capable of integrating history with scientific and personal experience.[31]

After examining the events of Christian history according to the disclosure-commitment schema,[32] in which the historical records mediate a discernment of their religious significance, Ramsey takes up the question of the criteria that are to be employed in the evaluation of Christian historical language. Within the fivefold pattern which he suggests, one can easily discern the influence of many of the emphases that have been set forth in the preceding sections and chapters. The concepts of mediated disclosure, personal models, and empirical fit, together with the emphasis on the functional relation between science and religion, all form the basic weave upon which this pattern is traced. As Ramsey himself summarises at the conclusion of his article:

'What we need . . . is a model for reasoning which makes religious assertions both relate to historical events and yet transcend them, and this, I have hinted, can be found in characteristically personal argumentation. Problems of history and of the gospels are problems which can be matched in the logic of personal relationships, and I have suggested that since the logic of the one can be a clue to the logic of the other, we are not without standards of reasonableness by which to judge between better and worse theological arguments.[33]

The first criterion in Ramsey's fivefold pattern for the evaluation of theological discourse is the existence of what he terms 'pro-factors which we recognise as the grounds'[34] for the initial belief that the event in question actually took place. If it is a question of whether or not a particular person is in love with another person, there must be certain actions and/or statements which ordinarily could be said to provide a reasonable basis for believing that such is the case. With regard to the question of whether or not the

119

Resurrection took place, Ramsey suggests that such factors as the empty tomb, the disciples' awe-struck reactions, the witness to post-Resurrection appearances, and Old Testament parallels all need to be taken into account.[35]

The second criterion pertains to the consistency with which the belief in question harmonises with the events and beliefs that both precede and follow from it. In the case of love, "There must be the possibility that this presupposition of love or trustworthiness harmonises with a vast area of X's behaviour towards me".[36] In the case of Christ's Resurrection, to continue with Ramsey's example, such things as his prior activities, teachings, and character, together with the succeeding generalisations and practices of the Christian church, are all relevant.[37]

Ramsey's third criterion involves the consideration of 'contra-factors' which might militate against the initial belief. Although the consideration of such factors when they arise is necessary to balance the initial pro-factors, their existence 'will not, by itself, invalidate our presupposition'.[38] Again, in the case of Resurrection-belief, the possibility that someone stole the body, and 'the general scientific quest for regularities'[39] deserve serious negative weight. However, as Ramsey's analyses of miracles and the scientific method have shown, whether or not a particular event has occurred cannot be determined strictly on the basis of past regularities.

In connection with this third criterion, Ramsey makes a fourth point which places him squarely in the empiricist tradition. After warning against rejecting any particular belief solely on the basis of contra-factors, he says:

> 'Even so, there must certainly be the logical possibility of rejecting our presupposition if too many contra-factors come to light. Further, this logical possibility will remain even though the exact point when the presupposition will be rejected cannot be specified beforehand. Incidentally, in this connection it seems to me that, in what contemporary philosophers call the falsification controversy, religious people have been far too inclined to grant their opponents' interpretations of such phrases as "I will trust God though he slay me", as though religious belief could never entertain the possibility of critical contra-factors.'[40]

In reference to the question of the actuality of the Resurrection, Ramsey maintains that although 'we must be prepared to reject the Resurrection if too many contra-factors appear . . . we have no need to specify a point of rejection beforehand'.[41] In a word, there is a real sense in which religious beliefs are based on accumulative evidence and a weighing of opposing factors!

The final criterion that Ramsey mentions calls attention to the fact that often some of the initial pro-factors, which have given rise to a broadly corroborated belief, may later on prove to be bogus. 'But that, by itself, will not weaken our judgement of love or trustworthiness if, by that time, our wider perspective is sufficiently stable to incorporate it.'[42] This criterion requires that attention be given to the dynamic encompassing aspect of personal and/or religious belief. Christian faith may be reasonably maintained even if some of the initial causative factors must, upon later examination, be rejected; provided that a still broader experiential base has been constructed.[43]

The employment of the foregoing criteria in connection with the historical dimension of Christian faith is a specific instance of the application of Ramsey's concept of empirical fit to the question of religious confirmation. The criteria are complex and flexible; yet they are adequate to their purpose if conscientiously applied. It is true that they do not provide a 'slide rule guarantee' for an absolute distinction between the true and false in all religious questions. But neither does an engagement period in all cases of matrimony, nor a credit reference in all cases of bank loans. Nevertheless, in none of these areas of human experience is it necessary to conclude that there are no generally reliable standards, or that none are necessary.

'For if what I have been saying is right, it can be reasonable to base a full and total personal commitment on what may be no more than "a whisper" of a man's voice. But our commitment will only be reasonable if we strive continuously to get clearer and clearer about the spatio-temporal facts and their harmony one with another. Nor, because our commitment may be reasonably based on a few facts, do we reasonably or rightly conclude that it might just as well be based on none at all, or that no "facts" matter. We return in the end to what we were saying earlier—the Christian faith cannot be content merely with historical facts, nor can it do without them. But no more can love or trustworthiness or any "existential" human situation, be content to regard persons as no more than their overt behaviour. Neither can it seriously pretend that the love and trustworthiness could still exist if there were no visible behaviour at all.'[44]

This then is the way in which Ramsey understands the nature of religious confirmation. Religious beliefs and assertions, like their personal and historical counterparts, can and must be evaluated in terms of their general empirical fit. There is one other major emphasis in Ramsey's position on religious confirmation which needs to be treated before moving ahead to his view of religious knowledge in particular.

It can be seen from the main emphases and arguments of his position that Ramsey is convinced Christian theism can be vindicated as the most adequate view of human experience. On the basis of a proper understanding of experience in terms of disclosure-situations, and on the basis of a thorough interpretation of the various levels and functions of language, Ramsey concludes that theistic language is not only possible, but necessary. '. . . It is "God" which I believe . . . to be the integrator word which provides the most simple, far-reaching and coherent metaphysical map.'[45]

It must not be concluded, however, that he maintains Christian theism can be vindicated, by means of its superior empirical fit, in an entirely objective manner. Indeed, the very concept of empirical fit negates such a possibility. There is an implicit emphasis throughout Ramsey's writings on the necessity of active involvement as an important aspect of any confirmation process. This emphasis is implied by his contextual and dimensional approach to experience, by his insistence on the primacy of personal models, and by his adaptation of much of the scientific method to the concerns of religions.

This implicit emphasis, strange as it may seem, reflects a common foundational concern of both empiricism and existentialism. In spite of their many differences and conflicts, Ramsey constantly strives to preserve the element of experiential involvement which underlies both of these movements. The empiricist insists on the necessity of evaluating each and every belief by actually putting it to the test in terms of experiential results. The existentialist insists on the necessity of personal involvement as the ultimate criterion for determining the adequacy for belief. Judging from his basic emphases, it is sound to conclude that Ramsey thinks these two commitments are similar, if not identical.[46]

The most straightforward exposition that Ramsey offers of his understanding of the role of experiential involvement is found in 'A Logical Exploration of Some Christian Doctrines'.[47] After giving an analysis of several theological concepts in terms of his model-qualifier schema, Ramsey concludes his discussion of the Trinity by raising the following question: '. . . how shall we know when we have rightly understood the doctrine and when we have not? How shall we know when we have confessed a true faith?'[48] In other words, how does one test the truth of his theological models?

Although his answer to this general question is given in terms of the Trinitarian formula and its associated models in particular, it clearly expresses his position concerning the testing of theological models in general. In brief, 'The answer is that we only know, we only understand, Trinitarian theology as we retrace our steps, as we return from that Mount of Vision to which Trinitarian discourse should have led us, and prove our Trinitarian theology, in Trinitarian living'.[49] Ramsey goes on to explicate this answer by suggesting a parallel between it and Wittgenstein's emphasis upon looking for use instead of meaning. Rather than forcing theological language into a picture-theory mould which demands objects as referents for all terms, one ought to ascertain the logic and purpose of theological terms, and then see if they give rise to the disclosure which leads to the 'form of life' known as Christian worship and behaviour.[50]

Thus the final criterion for judging the worth of a theological model is the actual attempt to structure one's life according to the pattern which it presents. With respect to the Trinitarian model, Ramsey suggests that its value will be found to lie in its ability to bring together three strands of Christian experience. If this model enables one to integrate his awareness of God in creation and preservation in terms of the Father, his awareness of God's grace and redemption in terms of the Son, and his awareness of God's presence in personal relationships in terms of the Holy Spirit, then it will have been confirmed in the only possible and appropriate way. In actually putting the model to use, the twofold concern for evaluation and commitment are unified!

'Trinitarian Doctrine is . . . an endeavour, in terms of some model for unity, be it philosophical or homely, to unite the three strands of talking about God which characterise the Christian message; and to talk about these three strands in such a way that, while they are fulfilled in the mystery of the Triune God on the one hand, they are worked out in what might be called Trinitarian faith and behaviour on the other.'[51]

Ian Ramsey

3 RELIGIOUS KNOWLEDGE

In 1961–2 Ramsey delivered the Frederick D. Maurice lectures at King's College, London. Therein he dealt with the problem of religious knowledge as it relates to the thought of Frederick D. Maurice. Specifically, Ramsey examined Maurice's views on three main themes by way of developing a sound view of religious knowledge. The three themes were: the doctrine of eternal punishment, the foundation of Christian social ethics, and the nature of subscription to creeds and articles of faith. These lectures have been published in book form,[52] and I will use them as the primary source material for this final section of my presentation of Ramsey's position.

Ramsey begins by pointing up the importance, and the opposing positions, of the contemporary debate over the nature of religious knowledge. In one camp there are those, both religious and non-religious, who insist that the claims of religion are nothing if not certain. In the other camp there are those, again both religious and non-religious, who maintain that the claims of religion are entirely contingent and corrigible. Although this debate has ancient historical roots, Ramsey is convinced that it is of special significance in our day:

'Let us frankly face it, we are in a most serious intellectual crisis that requires a major operation, which will test both the sympathetic sensitiveness of the surgeons and their intellectual skills and techniques, if we are to come out of it alive ... even if philosophy no longer flourishes the nonsense veto which it did in the 'thirties, nevertheless it still presents us with a challenge—a challenge to religious people to elucidate the empirical anchorage of their religious assertions.'[53]

After discussing and quoting at some length Maurice's views on the doctrine of eternal punishment, Ramsey gives his own analysis of the basis and linguistic logic of the concept. What he finds of value in Maurice's treatment is the emphasis on the centrality and uniqueness of the term 'eternal'. Not only did Maurice think that this term, in all its many uses, is a key word in the New Testament, but he was aware of its peculiar logic as well. In brief, he maintained that this term qualified the term 'punishment' in such a way as to free it from its normal experiential connotations. This interpretation obviated the more traditional one by insisting that 'eternal' has a qualitative, rather than a quantitative (temporal) function. Maurice concluded that 'eternal punishment' was logically equivalent to 'Divine punishment' which calls attention to the kind (not the length) of punishment involved—namely that administered by the loving Heavenly Father.[54]

Obviously Maurice's analysis is but a contemporary idiom away from the heart of Ramsey's own analysis. Ramsey proceeds to discuss the model-qualifier pattern of the phrase 'eternal punishment' by way of emphasising that its primary purpose is to call attention to, and map the logic of, the disclosure of God's loving consistency in dealing with men as free moral agents. Here again he stresses the importance of being circumspect when tracing the pattern of theological phrases in order to avoid logical and religious blunders.[55] 'Punishment' anchors the doctrine in empirical experience, while 'eternal' indicates that 'punishment' is to be taken in a way that is appropriate to the nature of God the Father. Unfortunately, this qualification has often been overlooked when it has been 'supposed that people like Milton and Dante have produced the colour slides (so to say) of a future world tour.'[56]

At the close of this lecture, and on the basis of its content, Ramsey sets forth his essential thesis concerning religious knowledge in general and Christian knowledge in particular. He distinguishes between the experiential knowledge of God Himself, which is certain to the person involved, and the more theoretic knowledge of God, which is always approximate and open to revision. The former is more of a tacit knowledge which, although it cannot be made explicit, is as certain as our knowledge of ourselves and other persons. The latter is the necessary, but always insufficient, attempt to be articulate about our experiential disclosures of the mystery of God. Ramsey's own statement of his thesis is extremely clear, and so I quote it at length:

'Let no one deny the need and usefulness of what we may call theological approximation to picturesque projections of—doctrine. There is nothing disreputable about them *provided that* we recognise them for the approximations they are. Further, if there is one principle to be borne in mind when making a comparative assessment of theological approximations, it is: the *more* we say, the more we need to be cautious about what we say . . . we can be sure of God, yet tentative about our theology. Let us frankly acknowledge theological uncertainties. Let us not conceal them

125

from our congregations or our audiences: let us not perpetuate schemes that demand or imply greater certainty than we possess. Still more, let us not build, on mistaken foundations, vast systems which suffocate religion. Let us acknowledge where at various points we are doctrinally "unsure" . . . recognising that it is *not* inconsistent to claim at the same time that we are sure of God—God given to us in a disclosure to which all our language can at best only lead, and which all our discursive theology will ever inadequately try to talk about, of which all our pictures are at best temporal projections.'[57]

By way of illustration, Ramsey offers a parallel case of being certain about what is discerned in a disclosure-situation without being able to be exhaustively articulate about it. In using this illustration he is careful to avoid implying that it is any more than simply an example which sheds some light upon his basic distinction. Upon considering a series of circles and their respective diameters, one may discern that there is an invariant ratio between the two. 'If so, we will be *sure* of π. But when we try to express this π in language which everyone will receive, we never reach beyond uncertainty—we have what might be called "numerical uncertainty".'[58] In other words, one can be sure that the ratio is invariant, while necessarily approximate in specifying what the ratio is. This same pattern can be seen to obtain in relationship to personal knowledge, in that we can be sure of the 'thatness' of ourselves and others, without being able to be certain of the 'whatness'. Our knowledge of God, on Ramsey's view, follows essentially the same pattern. Thus religious knowledge is seen to be of two kinds: tacit, experiential awareness, which is certain; and explicit, theoretic designation, which is tentative.

This same theme of a 'broader concept of reasonableness'[59] is carried through in Ramsey's second lecture on 'Christian Social Duty'. After presenting a rather detailed and most interesting discussion of the foundation of Christian ethics in relationship to past and present positions, a discussion which cannot be explored within the confines of this present study, Ramsey arrives at a similar conclusion. He is convinced that it is possible, indeed necessary, to be aware of one's duty without being able to specify, *a priori*, the contextual details. He thinks it is the theologian's task

'. . . to be expert in his own field, and to bring into play *not* one or two choice passages, or some particular slogan of a Reformation or counter-Reformation, *but* all and every element in the Christian dispensation that can be grist to the mill . . . for assuming that, or in so far as, these biblical narratives and classical references were themselves interlocked with a contemporary culture and social pattern, and in this wider context had their point, then there is reason to hope that this original point may now break in on us as we bring alongside our own particular situation.'[60]

Such a process will issue in a specific judgement for a particular context, and will have to be re-evaluated and modified as that context changes. 'Being sure in religion does not entail being certain in theology; to be aware of our Duty does not necessarily give us an infallible prescription. . . . Christian morality with all its reformable pronouncements is a permanent adventure. . . .'[61]

In the final lecture Ramsey discusses the ramifications of his distinction between religious knowledge and theological knowledge for the practice of subscribing to creeds and articles of faith.[62] After rejecting the possibility that such subscription, which is expressed by the phrase 'I believe . . .', could be a form of casual or hesitant belief, Ramsey asserts that:

'. . . credal questions were not of the form: Do you believe that so-and-so is the case? which is like: Is Charlie in fact in? Or, were my slippers in fact there? But they were of the form: do you believe in God, in Jesus Christ? which is more like: do you believe in, do you trust Charlie? Or, to my wife, do you trust me?'[63]

In this way Ramsey calls attention to the fact that baptismal creeds, such as the Apostles' Creed, place the term 'in', and not the term 'that', after the phrase 'I believe'. This move implicitly insures that the unique commitment-character of credal belief will be maintained. The primary force of the questions and answers employed in connection with baptism and worship services is, as with those employed in a wedding ceremony, that of personal commitment. In other words, the type of belief involved in this context is essentially religious in character, and does not imply any form of tentativeness whatsoever. It expresses thorough commitment to the religious dimension which has been disclosed to the participant.

It is absolutely essential not to mis-read Ramsey's distinction between 'belief in' and 'belief that' as a hard-and-fast separation.

Indeed, it is precisely against such a separation, which is all too popular today, that Ramsey directs much of his effort. The fact that the primary thrust, or purpose, of credal belief is to express commitment does not exclude it from having factual ramifications. In fact, as is the case in a wedding ceremony, expressions of commitment often necessarily imply factual situations. To make further use of the geometrical imagery which is essential to Ramsey's position, this point could be made by saying that different dimensions need not be mutually exclusive.

When one turns to what Ramsey terms 'conciliar creeds', the same general pattern is operative, but the primary force is different. With respect to such creeds as the Nicene, whose purpose was a consistent and thorough expression of Christian commitment, the factual dimension played a more important role.

> 'For example—"I believe in Jesus Christ". Certainly, he was a historical figure: a man who wept, who was hungry, who was crucified, suffered and buried. But to cope as well with utterances like those of the apostle Thomas, to allow for insights into the cosmic Christ, these historical phrases came to be balanced by others, by phrases from current philosophy which not only provided a consistent frame in which to set the biblical phrases but whose logic was peculiar enough to make their transcendent point; philosophical phrases such as: "being of one substance with the Father", "by whom all things were made".'[64]

It is in this way that Ramsey sees the difference between the various types of creeds and their corresponding belief-statements. Baptismal creeds and belief are grounded in religious experience and scriptural insights,[65] and thus focus on commitment, but not to the exclusion of cognition. Conciliar creeds and belief seek to integrate and unify religious statements into a rational pattern which reflects the categories and insights of their contemporary setting,[66] and thus they focus on cognition, but not to the exclusion of commitment. The latter are to be understood in terms of the model-qualifier pattern which Ramsey has suggested in other contexts. Unfortunately, a large part of church history bears witness to the fact that far too often these creeds were understood as 'descriptive blueprints of the life of God'.[67]

Ramsey is especially concerned to ferret out the confusions which have surrounded the interpretation of the Thirty-nine Articles of the Church of England, since he himself is a member of its clergy.

He locates the cause of the confusion in an uncircumspect understanding of the concept of 'literal meaning'.

> 'Undoubtedly, most people believed that the one true meaning of
> the Articles was some set of incontrovertible facts which the
> Articles pictured. The very possibility of contextual interpre-
> tations, and the new responsibility of judging between different
> and various contextual interpretations was hardly, if at all,
> recognised.'[68]

Ramsey's first point is that the phrase 'literal meaning', far from
necessitating a straightforward descriptive logic, insists rather on a
logic which is appropriate to the context within which the theological statement in question arose. The statement is interpreted
literally when it is interpreted according to the purpose and logic
of its 'natural home'. In a word, the emphasis on literal meaning
'is meant to guard against what is in fact intellectual dishonesty,
against anyone giving to a word or phrase a completely arbitrary
context'.[69] Ramsey's second point is that since such historical contexts differ from those of any given contemporary setting, there
is a constant need to re-think and re-state theological convictions
in language which both jibes with contemporary categories and
preserves the original purpose of credal statements.[70]

With such distinctions as the foregoing in mind, Ramsey turns to
the question of a revision of the Thirty-nine Articles.[71] Although
the Articles are similar to the conciliar creeds in that they seek to
map the logic of religious assertions in light of their respective
contemporary categories, they differ from the creeds in that they
are further removed from the historical and biblical sources.

> 'The Creeds are the first and classic essay in consistency and
> give us rules to guide all subsequent discourse; whereas the
> Articles can be seen as specimen discourse designed and developed
> to help teaching and exposition in certain historical circum-
> stances. Creeds and Articles are different in so far as they may
> be roughly compared in particular to the rules of the game, and
> the game itself.'[72]

In the light of these insights, Ramsey suggests that although there
is always work to be done in coming to a better historical and/or
contemporary understanding of the language and intent of the
articles of faith, the real challenge of today involves digging into

the logical and linguistic foundations of religious language and thought.

'. . . some of the most threatening of the intellectual battles the Christian has to fight are not from within but from the outside, and being not only cosmological but epistemological, even penetrate far enough to raise serious difficulties about the kind of appeal which Christians make or might wish to make to the Bible. Faced by these complex and intricate critical issues, what is needed is not more Articles, but much more preliminary under-labouring, much more spadework.'[73]

From all this discussion of the nature of 'subscription-faith', Ramsey draws his twofold conclusion concerning the nature of religious knowledge.[74] First, theological statements and knowledge, patterned as they are after a model-qualifier logic, must always be viewed as approximate and subject to revision. In brief, they must be understood as tentative. Such an approach not only frees Christian theology from the narrow confines of a static deductive system, but it enables Christian thinkers to unite proper humility with the thrill of theological discovery. Second, religious commitment and knowledge, based as they are in experiential disclosure-situations, must be viewed as sure and certain, even as are personal commitment and knowledge.

Once again it is important not to construe Ramsey's distinction between religious certitude and theological tentativeness as a thorough-going dichotomy. Not only is the major drive of his entire position contrary to such a dichotomy, but his present account explicity deals with these two elements in polar fashion, as 'a rhythm of faith and love with understanding'.[75] The tentativeness of theological assertions need not render one's religious commitment tentative, because the latter's basis is in a religious experience which gives rise to the former.

'My point then is that we are to be tentative, but always contextually tentative, about our theology, while grounding that theology in a disclosure of God. In this way we are to be sure in religion while being tentative, but contextually tentative in theology. This means that at each stage, the tentative is controlled by the context to date, so that we always assert something firmly and squarely in a context. But such assertions are always ripe for development.'[76]

130

This question of the relationship between religious certitude and theological tentativeness comes up again at the close of Ramsey's essay 'On the Possibility and Purpose of a Metaphysical Theology'.[77] Against popular philosophical opinion, Ramsey maintains that while our knowledge of our own existence in relation to another is incorrigible, each and every descriptive statement that encompasses and implies this knowledge is itself corrigible. Thus there is a distinction between the knowledge of self-awareness (e.g. 'I am'), which is incorrigible, and the knowledge of self-description (e.g. 'I am angry'), which is corrigible. Furthermore, since the knowledge of God and the use of the term 'God' are to be modelled after personal knowledge and the use of the term 'I' respectively, Ramsey concludes that a distinction between religious certitude and theological approximation can, and must, be made. 'Thus God is guaranteed to us very much as we are to ourselves. But no description is guaranteed. The basic assertion about God does not stand or fall on one or many particular verifiable assertions. Yet as with ourselves, so with God, intuition and description come together.'[78]

This 'coming together' of intuition, or incorrigible insight, and descriptive statement cannot, according to Ramsey, be classified as 'absolutely certain' nor as 'wholly corrigible'. He suggests that perhaps the best epistemological classification of such statements would be that of 'probable'—although this term is also subject to misunderstanding. He means the designation 'probable' to indicate a third classification between absolute certainty and absolute corrigibility which results from the conjunction of first-person phrases with descriptive statements. 'For it would be "probable" in Butler's sense, a sense which makes a "probable" utterance completely determinative of one's total behaviour.'[79]

Ramsey gives the following analysis of a first-person utterance by way of illustrating its epistemological structure: [80]

I have a headache
= There's a headache .... which is mine.
   (descriptive, corrigible; relating to 'objects')   (incorrigible)
= I exist .... with a headache.
   (incorrigible)   (corrigible)
|——————— 'probable' ———————|

Ramsey stresses the fact that the term 'probable' applies to the total statement and not to either of its components in isolation.

Thus, to revert to the terminology employed earlier in this section, when the dimensions of religious certitude and theological tentativeness are brought together in a single assertion, the resultant knowledge can be said to be probable in its nature. '. . . We might wish to regard "God exists" as formally indicative of the "incorrigible" element in any total theistic assertion'[81] while regarding what we predicate to God as the corrigible element.

In this way Ramsey seeks to avoid conceiving of God's existence as a probable scientific hypothesis, while maintaining the logical point of connection between the language of theism and empirical experience. One's knowledge of God, which arises out of a mediated disclosure of the divine dimension, is said to yield certitude. One's language about God, which is an attempt to be articulate about the divine mystery, is said to yield approximate knowledge. The combination of these two forms of knowledge, expressed in contextually qualified religious assertions, is said to yield probable knowledge. In all this, the model is personal knowledge of oneself and others.

This concludes my account of the final phase of Ramsey's implicit epistemological arc. In summary, this final phase began with Ramsey making two main points about the relation between science and religion: (1) they are similar in that science is more dependent upon disclosures and model-terms than is often realised, while religion is more dependent upon empirical anchorage and confirmation than is usually admitted; (2) they are dissimilar in that science seeks and finds precise experimental verification, while religion seeks and finds flexible experiential confirmation. The middle part of this final phase consists of Ramsey's analysis of the nature of model-thinking. After making a distinction between picturing models and analogue models within science and theology, he maintains that the latter, being functional and flexible in nature, are appropriate and adequate for religious language and knowledge. He then applies this functional and flexible standard to the problem of historical reasoning by way of suggesting criteria for the evaluation of Christian historical language. In all of this, the need for personal involvement is stressed. The last part of this final phase is summarised in the preceding paragraph.

All three of the phases of the epistemological arc formed by Ramsey's overall position have now been presented. Religious language has its basis in experiential disclosures of the religious dimension that are mediated through empirical situations and spatio-temporal facts. The primary model of this sort of disclosure is that involved in self-awareness. The over-arching pattern of religious language is that of the qualified model which establishes both the empirical anchorage and the unique logical status of God-talk. Here, too, the primary model is that of the term 'I'. The sort of knowledge which results from this view of religious language is twofold. One can be sure of the experientially mediated knowledge of God, while being tentative about every and all forms of theoretic knowledge of God's nature and activity. Such an approach justifies the title 'A Wider Empiricism'.

'Not the least merit of logical empiricism, then, is that it provides us with an inroad into theology which can break down misunderstandings, and by centring attention on to both language and "facts", can from the beginning hope to be both intellectually honest and devotionally helpful—a combination not always achieved.'[82]

NOTES

1 'Religion and Science: A Philosopher's Approach', *Church Quarterly Review*, CLXII (January–March 1961), p. 77. Also in *Christian Empiricism*, pp. 143–58.
2 *Religion and Science: Conflict and Synthesis*, p. 76.
3 ibid., p. 76.
4 'Religion and Science: A Philosopher's Approach', p. 79. Also in *Christian Empiricism*, p. 154.
5 ibid., pp. 83–4; *Christian Empiricism*, pp. 149–50.
6 ibid., p. 88; *Christian Empiricism*, p. 155.
7 ibid., pp. 90–1; *Christian Empiricism*, pp. 157–8.
8 ibid., p. 90; *Christian Empiricism*, p. 154.
9 *Religion and Science: Conflict and Synthesis*, p. 80.
10 'Religion and Science: A Philosopher's Approach', p. 91. Also in *Christian Empiricism*, p. 158.
11 Max Black, *Models and Metaphors*, pp. 219–43.
12 *Models and Mystery*, pp. 4–5.
13 ibid., pp. 6–7.
14 ibid., p. 21.
15 ibid., p. 13.
16 ibid., p. 14.
17 ibid., p. 16. Cf 'Towards the Relevant in Theological Language', *Modern Churchman*, VIII (September 1964), pp. 49–52.
18 ibid., p. 16.
19 ibid., pp. 16–17.
20 ibid., p. 17.
21 ibid., p. 38.
22 John Wild, 'Is There a World of Ordinary Language?' *Philosophical Review*, LXVII, no. 4 (October 1958), p. 460.

23 W. V. O. Quine, *Word and Object*, especially pp. 118–24, 233–8,
24 *Models and Mystery*, pp. 19–20.
25 ibid., p. 21.
26 ibid., p. 46.
27 Ian Ramsey, 'History and the Gospels: Some Philosophical Reflec
    Studia Evangelica III (Berlin), LXXXVIII (1964), p. 201. A
    Christian Empiricism, pp. 186–204.
28 ibid., pp. 202–3; *Christian Empiricism*, pp. 186–7.
29 This same position is set forth in more detail in Ramsey's eval
    of the debate between the followers of C. H. Dodd and Bultma
    Religious Language, pp. 107–21.
30 'History and the Gospels', p. 207; *Christian Empiricism*, p. 193.
31 ibid., p. 208; *Christian Empiricism*, p. 195.
32 ibid., pp. 211–12; *Christian Empiricism*, pp. 195–8.
33 ibid., p. 217; *Christian Empiricism*, p. 204.
34 ibid., p. 212; *Christian Empiricism*, p. 198.
35 ibid., p. 213; *Christian Empiricism*, p. 199.
36 ibid., p. 212; *Christian Empiricism*, p. 198
37 ibid., p. 213; *Christian Empiricism*, p. 199.
38 ibid., p. 212; *Christian Empiricism*, p. 198.
39 ibid., p. 213; *Christian Empiricism*, p. 199.
40 ibid., pp. 212–13; *Christian Empiricism*, pp. 198–9.
41 ibid., p. 213; *Christian Empiricism*, p. 199.
42 ibid., p. 213; *Christian Empiricism*, p. 199.
43 ibid., p. 214; *Christian Empiricism*, p. 200.
44 ibid., pp. 216–17; *Christian Empiricism*, p. 203.
45 *Prospect for Metaphysics*, p. 164.
46 Some of the relationships between these two types of commitmen
    explored in Ramsey's 'The Authority of the Church Today', *Aut
    and the Church*, ed. R. R. Williams, p. 61.
47 Ramsey, 'A Logical Exploration of Some Christian Doctrines', *CI
    Theological Seminary Register*, LIII, no. 5 (May 1963), pp. 26ff.
48 ibid., p. 39.
49 ibid., p. 39.
50 ibid., p. 39.
51 ibid., p. 40.
52 Ramsey, *On Being Sure in Religion*.
53 ibid., pp. 2–3.
54 F. D. Maurice, *Theological Essays*, p. 436.
55 *On Being Sure in Religion*, p. 16.
56 ibid., p. 20.
57 ibid., p. 23.
58 ibid., p. 24.
59 ibid., p. 27.
60 ibid., p. 35.
61 ibid., p. 47.
62 ibid., pp. 48ff.
63 ibid., p. 53.
64 ibid., p. 54.
65 ibid., p. 52.
66 ibid., p. 54.

67   ibid., p. 54.
68   ibid., pp. 58–9.
69   ibid., p. 63.
70   ibid., p. 71.
71   ibid., pp. 88–90.
72   ibid., p. 87.
73   ibid., p. 84.
74   ibid., pp. 88–90.
75   ibid., p. 89.
76   ibid., p. 90.
77   *Prospect for Metaphysics*, pp. 175–7.
78   ibid., p. 176.
79   ibid., p. 176.
80   ibid., p. 176.
81   ibid., p. 177.
82   *Religious Language*, p. 216.

Part Three

CONCLUSION

Chapter 6

A BRIEF APPRAISAL

I shall begin this final chapter by considering some early and briefer objections which have been raised against Ramsey's position, and then I shall move to an evaluation of three more thorough and recent critiques of his position. Although there are a few points which stand in need of clarification and supplementation, my general conclusion is that Bishop Ramsey has essentially met the challenge of logical empiricism.

1 EARLY CRITICISMS AND REPLIES

In this section I shall present the critical comments of Frederick Ferré, H. D. Lewis, and Ninian Smart together with Ramsey's reply to each of them. In addition, I shall discuss Ramsey's appraisal of the thought of Paul van Buren. Although all of these considerations will be given serious attention for their own sake, it is hoped that they will shed additional light upon the exact nature of Ramsey's position as well.

Ferré sees both similarities and differences between Ramsey's view and that of Willem Zuurdeeg.[1] He finds them similar in that they both emphasise the unique functions of theological discourse. He finds them different in that while Zuurdeeg stresses the non-logical and convictional nature of religious language, Ramsey stresses the relation between its unique logic and the commitment to which it gives rise. After giving an extremely brief (just over one page), and therefore very inadequate, presentation of Ramsey's view of religious disclosure and God-talk, Ferré turns to what he terms Ramsey's 'subjectivism'.

He begins by quoting what he takes to be Ramsey's main defence against this charge:

'There is no question of a characteristically religious situation being merely "emotional", if that word is thought to claim that the characteristic features we have been mentioning are entirely (in some sense or other) "subjective". Let us emphasise, without any possibility of misunderstanding, that all these situations . . . when they occur, have an *objective* reference and are, as all situations, *subject-object* in structure. When situations "come alive", or the "ice breaks", there is objective "depth" in these situations along with and alongside any subjective changes.'[2]

To this Ferré replies:

'Although Ramsey has here succeeded in "emphasising" his view, he has not advanced a step toward defending it. He fails to deal with illusions or the place of hallucination in experience. These, too, would no doubt be "subject-object" in structure; but would Ramsey be content to have "characteristically religious situations" considered in this light? He is quite correct in asserting that religious experience has a high degree of "intentionality" . . . but is he not confusing "experiencing-*as*-objective" with having experience *of* the objective?'[3]

This charge of subjectivism, especially when based upon an analysis of Ramsey's *Religious Language*, is heard fairly frequently. And, as a quotation from Ramsey himself will presently make clear, it is in a certain sense quite justified. Since Ramsey addresses himself to this objection more thoroughly in response to another critic, I will momentarily postpone an analysis of his reply. Nevertheless, it should be mentioned at this juncture that Ferré's criticism is, to some extent, based on a superficial understanding of Ramsey's position. Not only is this reflected in his sketchy one-page treatment of Ramsey's thought, but it is also quite obvious from the fact that *Religious Language* (1955) is the only source from which he draws. Although several of Ramsey's more explicit publications appeared after Ferré's book (1961), some other materials were available prior to Ferré's writing, including 'Miracles: An Exercise in Logical Mapwork' (1952) and *Freedom and Immortality* (1960).

H. D. Lewis, after expressing confusion concerning Ramsey's analysis of freedom and immortality, also focuses on the problem of the objective reference of disclosure experiences.[4] With respect to the former confusions, he states that he is not clear as to the basis of Ramsey's argument for the logical primitiveness of personal freedom, and that he finds Ramsey's account of immortality philosophically and religiously inadequate. I will summarise Ramsey's reply[5] to these two points before returning to the problem of disclosures and their objectivity.

Concerning freedom, Ramsey replies by reiterating his belief that, although personal freedom cannot be derived as the conclusion of a factual or logical argument, it can be shown to be an implicit and necessary assumption of all human language and action by examining examples of routine situations which 'come alive' under certain circumstances. In these situations, one is aware of his selfhood and his freedom, even though he is unable to fully articulate this awareness. To borrow an idiom from Wittgenstein, and that not inappropriately, Ramsey maintains that there are realities which, although they cannot be 'said', can be 'seen'. 'Don't think; look.' In this way the argument for freewill can be seen to function as a pointer toward a personal disclosure.

Concerning immortality, Ramsey stresses the fact that his purpose was not to produce arguments for the actuality of immortality, but rather to show how its possibility can be empirically based in the realisation that we are more than the sum of our bodily behaviour. He finds that this realisation points up the transcendent, rather than the enduring, nature of selfhood, and thus makes it possible to conceive of transcending the death of the body. It is the unique logic of the first person pronoun that renders this concept philosophically defensible in a way that traditional talk about a 'thing-like' soul is not. Ramsey finds it religiously superior as well, since it is more in line with the New Testament concept of 'eternal life'.

With regard to Lewis's criticism that his religious disclosures would seem to have no objective referent, Ramsey offers a threefold reply. First, he states that he developed his concept of disclosure in order to indicate the empirical grounding of talk which is not merely descriptive. By the nature of the case, this type of discourse has an 'evocative use so that we shall only know what it means [i.e. what it talks about] when *inter alia* a disclosure has occurred'.[6] Second, Ramsey maintains that in one sense the referent of disclosure experiences will vary, as is the case with all experiences. What is disclosed will depend upon the epistemological object and the surrounding context. Mathematical contexts may disclose such objects as circles, cubes, and π, while moral and interpersonal contexts may disclose such things as duty and persons. In the same way, God and His activity may be disclosed by means of personal and historical contexts.[7] Third, Ramsey acknowledges that any particular disclosure-claim may well turn out to be what is often termed a 'subjective experience'. However, he insists that, as is the case with other initially peculiar experiences, a widening of the experiential context may actually substantiate the objectivity of the disclosure-claim.

> 'So while I agree that from the standpoint of first stage discourse disclosures disclose "anything", that does not preclude us from giving wider and wider interpretations, from supplying supplementary interpretations to characterise the object of the disclosure more reliably, as the context is progressively extended.'[8]

More thorough criticisms of Ramsey's position are offered by Ninian Smart. Although he registers these criticisms in more than one place,[9] there is one particular article which expresses his most complete critical attack,[10] and I shall focus upon it at this time. In addition to several minor objections, Smart levels three major and related criticisms against Ramsey's views. On the basis of these criticisms he concludes that Ramsey is essentially a non-cognitivist with regard to the nature of religious language. Calling attention to the fact that Paul van Buren[11] relies heavily upon Ramsey's writings, Smart asserts that Ramsey's position is at best compatible with existentialism, and at worst compatible with atheism. Obviously, Smart is unhappy with either alternative.

Smart's first major criticism is, along with Ferré and Lewis, that Ramsey's concept of disclosure dispenses with the element of transcendence. This, on Smart's view, not only does away with the possibility of an epistemological object, but obviates the whole point of religion. If religious experience does not put one in contact with a reality which transcends himself, why call it religious? His second major criticism points up the other side of the coin of subjectivism: Ramsey's position fails to provide a criterion for distinguishing between the real and the unreal on the experiential level, or between the true and the false on the linguistic level. What are the earmarks of an authentic disclosure and a reliable model? Finally, Smart emphasises the difficulties involved in attempting to move from self-awareness and 'I'-talk to God-awareness and God-talk. Although the former categories are known and used by nearly everyone, so that the existence of their object is not in question, the latter categories are not known and used by everyone, and thus the existence of their object is in question.

Ramsey's reply to Smart's criticism is a threefold one.[12] He begins by indicating that his *Religious Language*, which is the sole object of Smart's attack, was written early (1955) in the debate over the nature of religious language. At that time Ramsey claims he was striving to fulfil two purposes: (1) to show the complex and flexible richness of religious language, and (2) to show the actual broadness of empirical experience. Both of these purposes were aimed at overcoming the narrow outlook of those who were participating in the debate, such as Anthony Flew. Next, Ramsey indicates that since that time he has written quite widely, and often with the specific problems of objective confirmation and transcendence directly in view. As should be clear from a reading of Chapter Five of this present study, his *Models and Mystery*, which develops the concept of empirical fit, and his *On Being Sure in Religion*, which offers a theory of religious knowledge, speak quite clearly on these points. The same is true of his writings which deal with the nature of scientific and historical reasoning. This question of objectivity will be taken up again shortly.

Finally, Ramsey suggests that the subject-object distinction lying at the heart of the criticism that his view opens the door to subjectivism is itself in need of a thorough overhaul. He maintains that this distinction, while in a way necessary and helpful, is most often interpreted in such a way as to be dependent upon a questionable conceptual scheme, that is, one that implies that all objectivity is physical-object-objectivity. He implies that his own account of disclosures, which draws heavily upon the notion of mediated and tacit awareness, is based on a broader, and hence more adequate, interpretation of experience.

Ramsey summarises his reply to the criticism that his approach is lethal to theism in the following clever, but none the less pointed, manner:

'Here are admittedly complicated issues, and I agree that in *Religious Language* I hardly faced these questions of reference and criteria. Professor Smart is undoubtedly right to focus attention on this problem of objectivity and reference as being crucial in contemporary philosophical theology. But it will not be solved by rehashing—with or without curry—views of ontology and experience which have already proved only too attractive for "cultured despisers" like Flew. Meanwhile, I have no desire to be a purveyor of anodynes, lethal or other, and I hope that those who are still alive after reading *Religious Language* will perhaps

143

now turn to what I have written further on these points—not that I suppose that even now the matter is altogether satisfactorily worked out, but at least the reasons may become more evident why I consider it to be more exciting than true to call me an atheist.'[13]

In another publication[14] to which Ramsey contributes a chapter entitled 'Talking About God: Models, Ancient, and Modern', he has sought even more directly to meet the criticism that his position fails to provide an objective referent for God-talk. As will become apparent, this more recent handling of the problem is in actuality an extension of his earlier position as it has been discussed in Chapter Five. His main point is that in a religious disclosure one is aware of being confronted by a dimension of reality which breaks in on one's consciousness in much the same way as one is faced with a moral claim.

'It is, I hope, evident that on this view when we appeal to "cosmic disclosures" we are not just talking about ourselves, nor merely of our own "experience", we are not just appealing to our own private way of looking at the world. If that were so, then the appeal to cosmic disclosures would be a scarcely-veiled form of atheism, which is what Professor Ninian Smart supposes to be the case. On the contrary a cosmic disclosure reveals something of whose existence we are aware precisely because we are aware of *being* confronted. Indeed we speak of a disclosure precisely when we acknowledge such a confrontation, something declaring itself to us, something relatively active when we are relatively passive.'[15]

Further on in this same publication, Ramsey offers two sets of criteria for ranking and evaluating the various models for speaking of God. The first set pertains to a model's 'justifying itself as far as it can alongside other models'.[16] Herein one ranks models according to their ability to balance with, or include, one another. The more harmonious and inclusive, the better the model. The second set of criteria pertains to Ramsey's concept of 'empirical fit', and may in fact disqualify a model which has passed 'muster' in regard to the first set just mentioned. 'The kind of empirical fit which provides a second set of criteria for preferences between models is much more like the kind of fit which detectives look for between certain new clues and a "theory" of the crime with which they are provisionally working.'[17]

After making these two general points about the objectivity of disclosures and the criteria for evaluating God-models, Ramsey addresses himself to the question of why the term 'God' should be employed in connection with these disclosures and models. He begins by developing a parallel case with respect to the use of the term 'circle' as it might be employed in connection with the disclosure arising from a consideration of a series of polygons with an ever increasing number of sides. Although another term (say 'x') might very well be used in such a situation, especially if the disclosure were evoked among persons who were unacquainted with the term 'circle', when the two terms are brought alongside of one another it would become apparent that they were being used to map the same dimension of experience. Thus they could be equated with one another. Ramsey concludes:

'Now in the same way, we might choose to call what a cosmic disclosure discloses as "X", and we have already seen that there could be good grounds for belief in "one X". Further, we would then talk about X in terms of any model which the various routes to a cosmic disclosure provided; and we would talk the more reasonably about X, in terms of this one model, the longer it had been cautiously developed under checks and balances, which amounts to saying the greater the number of models which has been incorporated into our discourse. Any one model would enable us to be articulate about X, in some way or another, but if we wanted to talk as adequately as possible about X we would build out the most consistent, comprehensive, coherent and simple discourse from as many models as possible. Now, if we did this, my contention is that we would see a language emerging which fitted closer and closer to the language which a believer uses about God, and because of this increasing fit, the further we go, the more reasonably we would then conclude "For X, read God", and the more reasonably would we talk of the models being models of God, and of the cosmic disclosure disclosing God.'[18]

Such comments should suffice to lay to rest permanently the charge that Ramsey's position makes no provision for the objectivity-claim of Christian language. For the sake of thoroughness, however, it can also be noted that this same point is developed somewhat differently by Ramsey in *Christian Discourse*, where he says:

145

'*It is the objectivity of what declares itself to us*—challenges us in a way that *persons may do*. It is in this sense that God declares his objectivity, and some would say that in a similar sense Duty also declares its objectivity. It is to talk of God's objectivity in this sense that personal and impersonal models are used.

'To put it otherwise. We reach *some* "facts" by selection and pointing them out—and for some purposes and in some contexts we can even "pick out" persons. But we reach *other* "facts" by their disclosing themselves to us, challenging us—and these are such facts as the "fact" of Duty, of the Moral Law, or of persons.'[19]

The only significant criticism which Ramsey fails to respond to directly is Smart's concern over moving from talk about the logic and 'transcendental' implications of 'I' to talk about the logic and 'transcendental' implications of 'God'. It will be recalled that Smart objected that while there is little, or no, debate about the reality of individual selves, there is a good deal of debate about the reality of God. Although he does not reply directly to this criticism, there seem to me to be two answers inherent within Ramsey's overall approach that bear mentioning. First, one aspect of Ramsey's analysis of the relationship between these two terms is strictly logical in character, and thus is not to be construed as an argument from the reality of the self to the reality of God. The fact remains that the logic of the two terms is very similar and Ramsey's analysis has shown this to be the case. Moreover, there is a sense in which Ramsey claims that in any situation which gives rise to an awareness of personal transcendence there must necessarily be a corresponding transcendence in the situation itself, to which the former is merely a response.

Second, although it is true that the reality of God is doubted by a large number of persons today, this was not always the case. In fact, in terms of sheer numbers, one could argue that those who doubt the existence of God are still in the minority. More important, however, is the fact that both the concept of God and His reality are part of the fabric of almost every culture, past or present. Indeed, there are those who would argue that although contemporary Western man is increasingly atheistic on the explicit level, his inability to shake himself free from the concept of God betrays the fact that he is still, and must always be, theistic on the tacit level. The ubiquity of the notion of God shows itself, if often in a negative form, in nearly every phase of Western culture from

A Brief Appraisal

articles in leading philosophical journals on the 'classical proofs' of God's existence to the films of Ingmar Bergman. The concept of God is not as obsolete nor problematic as Smart seems to think.

To come at the whole question from another direction, Ninian Smart's mentioning of Paul van Buren's reliance on Ramsey's thought, in van Buren's *The Secular Meaning of the Gospel*,[20] raises a most interesting issue. Whatever one may think of this book, it cannot be denied that in many ways it has become, for better or worse, the symbol of a 'new' approach to philosophical theology. Although this is not the place to enter into an analysis or evaluation of van Buren's views, one of his most glaring mistakes is the use he makes of Ramsey's insights. Unfortunately, however, the thought of these two thinkers is very often equated.

The differences between Ramsey's position and that of van Buren are partially brought out in their contributions to a symposium on the implications of the new philosophical theology for religious education. In the lead article[21] van Buren recasts the main theses of his book in terms of the issues of religious education. Once again he stresses the importance of discarding the traditional interpretation of theology as a metaphysical science. Thus, he emphasises, the goal of religious education is to provide the learner with a new way of looking at things, rather than with a system of doctrine. This new perspective should focus on faith and love as qualities of a new way of living—after the pattern of Jesus. In a word, van Buren seems to combine the 'blik-view' of R. M. Hare with the 'convictional view' of Willem Zuurdeeg. In this way he seeks to unite the insights of empiricism and existentialism.

Ramsey begins his response[22] to van Buren's position by agreeing with him that theology can no longer be viewed as a super-science, and that religious education must emphasise commitment and a life of love. On the other hand, Ramsey strongly objects to the subjective and non-transcendent tone of van Buren's approach:

'Christian education on my view is *not* the teaching of "a new way of looking at things" where it is supposed that everything except ourselves remains the same. For the "new way of looking at things" only occurs when these things themselves generate a disclosure. . . . It is this element of objectivity and transcendence which I am not sure that van Buren acknowledges or perhaps wishes to acknowledge.'[23]

147

In this way Ramsey seeks to differentiate his own position from that of van Buren on the basis of precisely those issues which others have used in seeking to identify the two positions. Moreover, in this indirect fashion, Ramsey replies to those critics who have accused him of failing to provide any objective basis and criteria for religious disclosure and language. He especially singles out the importance of the historical dimension of Christian faith.

> 'Christian stories must be so told in Christian education that while as a *sine qua non* they lead to disclosures, and while even a secular world may value them for the commitment they create, they also arise out of historical events that not only safeguard the relevance of the theology in terms of what the disclosures are explicated, but ensure also a reference to that element of transcendence without which the good news is less good than it might be.'[24]

Ramsey concludes by maintaining that while we need more (and not less) of van Buren, we need more of God as well! Unfortunately, in his response to the other contributors, van Buren fails to make any mention of Ramsey's specific comments.

2 RECENT CRITIQUES

I shall turn now to a consideration of three more recent critiques of Ramsey's views. Although there are other critical treatments of his work, the three discussed here seem to me to be the more important. Donald Evans has published a long, two-part article entitled 'Ian Ramsey on Talk About God', and I shall begin with it.[25]

Evans seeks to construct an overall picture of Ramsey's scattered and generally shorter works, because he hopes in this way to highlight both the strengths and the weaknesses of his position more clearly. Evans's article is a most helpful, if brief, survey of the major themes of Ramsey's thought, presented in an insightful and logical manner. In part one he moves from Ramsey's basic concern to develop 'a wider empiricism', through his account of "cosmic disclosures", to a discussion of the parallels between 'I' and 'God'. In the second part of his article, Evans focuses on Ramsey's concepts of God and transcendence as they relate to the notions of 'disclosure' and 'qualified models' respectively.

The critical strong points of Evans's account are three in number.

First, he sees and clarifies the relationship between Ramsey's thought and that of W. V. O. Quine, both in terms of their mutual concern for broadening empiricism, and in terms of their mutual acknowledgement of the necessity of 'irreducible posits' in any language-game. Second, Evans sees and clarifies the relationship between Ramsey and the Thomistic tradition, especially as it is reflected in the work of Austin Farrer. Both stress activity as the primary clue to knowledge of the divine, and both, although by means of quite differing vocabularies, develop a kind of hierarchy of concepts leading to a disclosure of God. Third, Evans's synthesising account offsets the impression, often gleaned from reading any one of Ramsey's works, that the latter has overlooked important considerations. When taken as a whole, Ramsey's literary corpus reveals that his overall position is remarkably thorough and consistent.

Evans's criticisms of Ramsey tend to focus on one major area, that of the criteria for determining 'empirical fit', or in Evans's words, 'the issue of rational preference'.

'The issue of rational preference also arises in Ramsey's presentation of negating and perfecting qualifiers. We may well ask for his basis for judging one human trait or activity as an imperfection, not to be ascribed to God at all, and another as a relative perfection, which can point towards God. For example, on what basis does he set aside some kinds of punishment as inappropriate, and select a punishment which expresses a reconciling love which overcomes separation? Or when he considers "God is impassible" and sets aside anything that changes, on what basis does he assume that change is an imperfection? Why not, as in much modern theology, a changing God as the ideal for changing man? Or when he applies "infinitely" to loving, and tells us to "think away any imperfect, finite, limited features", how does he know what counts as an imperfection in love? For example, is *need* for the loved one an imperfection or a relative perfection?'[26]

Evans accurately answers his own questions by pointing out that Ramsey appeals to three sorts of criteria: (1) Christian tradition, (2) metaphysical criteria, and (3) human experience. He then goes on to suggest that

'. . . it seems to me that the issues concerning rational preference (and indeed a great deal else in Ramsey's account of religious language), would be illuminated if Ramsey were to deepen his account of human experience by focusing explicitly on the question "What are our most significant insights concerning *man*?" For Ramsey's interpretation of talk about God depends a great deal on what he believes about man, his conception of human trust, wonder, hope, commitment, love and integrity. Ramsey's philosophical theology needs a more profound philosophical anthropology. . . .'[27]

My only comments about Evans's questions and suggestions are these. He is certainly correct in locating the crucial epistemological hinge in Ramsey's philosophy of religion, and in contending that much more work remains to be done at this point. At the same time, however, it should not go unnoticed that such development is not out of harmony with the general character and direction of Ramsey's perspective. Moreover, one hopes that by this time of day it is no longer necessary to argue the case that 'justifications come to an end'. If the demand is for reasonable clarity of criteria and responsible belief, then certainly Ramsey has provided an excellent starting-point—as Evans himself stresses. If, however, the demand is for absolute clarity and necessary knowledge, then one needs to go back to square one for a refresher course on 'a wider empiricism'.

This brings us to another recent critique of Ramsey's thought, that of Cynthia B. Cohen in her article 'The Logic of Religious Language'.[28] For, while providing many helpful insights into Ramsey's position, Cohen essentially makes unjustified demands of it. She argues that in stressing the evocative function of religious language, as opposed to its descriptive function, Ramsey has assumed that if terms do not have a physical referent they at least must have a non-physical referent. After giving examples of phrases which have meaning without reference, she states:

'We cannot define solely by intuitions of situations which "go beyond" the perceived, but must become involved in analysis and judgement to evolve a satisfactory definition. To have some definition of, say, "perfection", is not to know what a particular example of a perfect thing is, but to know what it is for something to be perfect. This form of definition is dependent on reflection and judgement about a term whose meaning may be intuitively clear enough initially so that we are able to recognise

150

particular examples. Analysis of this initial intuitive meaning enables us to form some concept of it and to apply the term consistently according to some principles.

'Ramsey must consider developing a theory of the meaning of terms which recognises that such meaning is a somewhat indeterminate conscious associate of the terms rather than an identifiable object open to intuitive grasp.'[29]

Cohen then moves on to argue that Ramsey's characterisation of religious language as evocative, since its meanings are not derived from conceptual analysis, renders it so subjective as to be without criteria of application. This is said to undermine Ramsey's own notion of empirical fit. What Cohen seems to suggest is that Ramsey ought (1) to 'own up' to the descriptive aspect of religious utterances, and (2) work out more systematic definitions for key religious terms. She concludes:

'I have suggested that Ramsey has made the meaning of ordinary words so extraordinary as to leave only a tenuous connection with their usual meaning. He has misconstrued their descriptive meaning and then has imposed on them an evocative function that is merely a means of intuitive association working according to no intelligible principles. The subtle and often equivocal constructions found within all kinds of religious discourse, and not just that of Christianity, must be analysed more completely if it is to be maintained that they reflect our religious experience and the nature of the religious object. The diverse epistemological strands of religious discourse which are brought together in the language of various religious traditions must be more clearly distinguished and explained. If the basis of all religious conceptions and language expressing these is an ontological insight into an object which "goes beyond" the perceived, such insight must be more carefully reinforced by an adequate theory of models.'[30]

There are two specific senses in which Cohen can be said to place unjustified demands on Ramsey's view of the meaning of religious utterances. First, she scolds him for making faulty assumptions about the nature of definitions while operating on highly questionable definitional assumptions of her own. Although she maintains that Ramsey has misunderstood Wittgenstein, Cohen's demand for a 'concept' of the meaning of any particular term which can be applied 'consistently according to some principles', together

151

with her remark that meaning is 'a somewhat indeterminate conscious associate' of terms, clearly indicates not only an unWittgensteinian bias, but a highly debatable view of the relation between definitions and meaning. Not only is Ramsey's approach more akin to Wittgenstein's concern for use in context, but it is more in harmony with the variety and richness of religious utterances than is an approach which seeks to reduce meaning to concepts and principles.

A second sense in which Cohen can be said to place unwarranted demands on Ramsey's position pertains to her claim that in his development of the evocative function of religious statements he has jettisoned any concern for their descriptive function, thus falling back into a kind of subjective intuitionism. This is unwarranted on two counts. It completely overlooks the extent to which Ramsey's account of language stresses its simultaneously multidimensional character. He is concerned to show that religious language is not *merely* descriptive. This does not deny that it has a descriptive dimension to it. This is, after all, the whole point of his extensive treatment of models and empirical fit. Furthermore, the meaning and truth of religious talk is not, in Ramsey's view, derived by intuition in a subjective manner. He seeks to ground them in a broad base of well-established usage and experience within the community of persons who find religious talk important. I must conclude that, at important junctures, Cohen has badly misunderstood Ramsey.

In my judgement F. Michael McLain offers a most penetrating and constructive critique of a crucial aspect of Ramsey's thought in his article 'From Odd-Talk to God-Talk?'.[31] While impressed with the effort to draw parallels between the logic of the words 'I' and 'God', McLain contends that Ramsey has drawn them ineptly, thereby producing an epistemological model which confuses our understanding of both self-knowledge and knowledge of God. Although McLain is in sympathy with Ramsey's concern to overcome the positivistic account of self-knowledge (whether Hume's or Ryle's), he argues that Ramsey has reverted to an incipient Cartesianism when he distinguishes too sharply between what Wittgenstein termed the 'subject' and the 'object' uses of 'I'.

In review, McLain sees Ramsey as maintaining that the reflexive quality of 'I' (the 'subject' use) gives witness to the 'inner' or 'private' dimension of the self known only by each speaker or individual subject. This self is always 'more' than the sum total of observable behaviour, or the objective self. Thus the logic of 'I' is 'odd' in that it systematically eludes objectification. McLain then traces Ramsey's analogical move from 'I'-talk to God-talk. Just as 'I'-talk is none the less legitimate for systematically eluding objectification, so God-talk need not be rejected because it has a similar logic. Moreover, McLain continues, it now becomes possible to speak of knowing God in much the same way as we speak of knowing ourselves, namely by 'disclosure'; mediated in and through objective events in the world without being reducible to them.

In turning from exposition to criticism, McLain focuses his position in this fashion:

> 'I agree that the appropriate *pièce de résistance* has been located; it is the self or the "I", and it is the self's uniqueness which must be explained. The strategy adopted by Ramsey . . . is to speak of an "experience", or "awareness", or "feeling", of the self, which, unlike any other experience, awareness or feeling, is private, and indescribable or non-linguifiable, that is, not capable of expression in spatio-temporal, perceptual categories. I shall try to show, however, that the strategy is misconceived for at least two reasons. First of all, insoluble dilemmas are created by depicting the "experience" we have of our "true" or "real" self as simply the opposite, point for point, of what is usually taken as the standard instance of "experience", viz., perceptual experience. Secondly, the programme is to secure an analogy to "God"; but how can something which is itself utterly mysterious serve as an analogy for anything?'[32]

Specifically, McLain has two complaints. The first is that in seeking to show that, contra Hume *et al.*, the self is in some sense transcendent to its behaviour, Ramsey overemphasises the 'unspeakable' character of self-knowledge. To put it differently McLain maintains that Ramsey really only envisions two kinds of language-games, the objectifying language of observables and the subjective language of unobservables. This dichotomy limits knowledge to the former while shrouding the latter in mystery. In contrast, McLain argues that self-knowledge, focusing in intentionality, while not expressible in so-called 'objectifying' language, is none the less expressible in the language of intentions. This expressibility renders self-knowledge and knowledge of other selves seemingly attendant to Ramsey's way of putting the matter. McLain concludes:

> 'I have not wished, in my remarks, to contest the legitimate sense in which persons can be termed a mystery; the unity of the self,

for instance, can only be apprehended, not described. This does not mean, however, that the self is altogether indescribable, or that it is inaccessible to observers. It is a mistake to insist that the self must be placed either among perceptible objects or mysterious subjects, a mistake committed both by Ramsey and . . . several of the existentialists. What is required to break this impasse is a set of categories that can make it clear that the self is not just a collection of observable phenomena and yet that do not render unintelligible or unimportant the self's relationship to itself, its knowledge of other persons, its irreducible embodiment, in short, the features of it which may be described without objectifying it. I have claimed that the categories of intention and action designate the area of the self which may be described or 'linguified' without objectifying it, though I do not suppose that I have established my theses concerning intentional activity.'[33]

McLain's second complaint about the way Ramsey treats the relation between 'I'-talk and God-talk pertains to its theological implications. He contends that, once the self has been shrouded in as much mystery as Ramsey urges, it becomes useless to draw parallels from the logic of talk about the self to the logic of talk about God. For since nothing can be said about the former without becoming entangled in misleading objectification, nothing can be said about the latter either. And so, the parallel hardly seems worth drawing. In MacLain's words:

'The need for an adequate account of the self is not a trivial matter for theology. Much contemporary theology and philosophy of religion has thought it enough to distinguish a realm of mystery from the realm of observables; the self and God are lumped together then as mysterious in the same sense. This is not sufficient. One cannot hold both that the self and God are equally mysterious, and that the former is the clue to the latter. To claim that the self is such a clue is to imply our relative certainty as to its nature; it is to suggest that we can specify the sense in which the I is like and unlike God.'[34]

McLain concludes his essay by suggesting that more than linguistic considerations are necessary to do theology, and by offering a brief analysis of how the notion of *activity*, as a 'metaphysical category', fits within the language-game of 'I'-talk about intentions and thereby provides a point of epistemological connection with God-talk. This, however, is not the place to pursue McLain's point of view. I shall now try to respond to his criticisms from Ramsey's perspective.

First, there is considerable force in McLain's criticisms and merit in his suggestions. Especially in his earlier writings, Ramsey did overplay the contrast between the public and the private self. To the extent that he did so, McLain's critique of his analysis of 'I'-talk and self-knowledge is on the mark. To put it the other way around, it would have greatly strengthened Ramsey's position had he given more attention to the positive dimension of the nature of self-knowledge. More specifically, as McLain points out, Ramsey often made frequent use of such terms as 'feeling' and 'experience' when discussing self-awareness, thus implying a subjective inaccessibility.

On the other hand, it must be noted that McLain has focused on an essay in which Ramsey sought to accomplish a negative task, namely to show the inadequacies of Gilbert Ryle's treatment of 'I'-talk and self-knowledge. His primary concern was not the development of his own view. Yet even in that essay he did use, as McLain acknowledges but never comments on, the same term McLain himself suggests as providing a key to self-knowledge and knowledge of God, namely the term 'action'. Moreover, in the same essay Ramsey also stressed the mediated character of self-awareness, so as to guard against the very 'privileged access' difficulties McLain accuses him of. I discussed both of these points on page 86.

More importantly, I would argue that the whole tenor of Ramsey's position is in basic accord with the thrust of McLain's critique. Ramsey sought at every juncture to define a position between any sort of behaviourism on the one hand and all forms of Cartesianism on the other. A consideration of his various analyses of the notion of disclosure makes this more than evident, for therein he consistently stresses the mediated character of awareness such that its object is more than, but never separable from, public factors. This holds true of self-awareness as well, and thus for Ramsey our knowledge of persons is clearly neither completely independent of behaviour nor 'utterly mysterious' as McLain asserts in my first quotation from his article. Chapter Three of the present work makes this point repeatedly.

Along the same vein, Ramsey's treatment of talk and knowledge of God heavily emphasises the importance of functional and/or

Ian Ramsey

activity models as opposed to substance and/or attribute models. Sections Two and Three of Chapter Four of this book clarify this point. This is essentially the same concern that McLain expresses, although admittedly from a slightly different angle. Once again, while I think McLain's points are well taken, I do not think that they are at odds with the overall character of Ramsey's work. That Ramsey's thought was moving in the direction of a more careful exploration of intentionality and activity can be seen by examining two of his most recent publications, *Models for Divine Activity*[35] and 'Facts and Disclosures'.[36] Further exploration of these issues would have greatly strengthened his position.

NOTES

1 Frederick Ferré, *Language, Logic and God*, pp. 137–45.
2 *Religious Language*, pp. 27–8.
3 *Language, Logic and God*, p. 141.
4 H. D. Lewis, 'Freedom and Immortality: A Review', *Hibbert Journal*, LIX (January 1961). Also in *Christian Empiricism*, pp. 207–18.
5 'Some Further Reflections on *Freedom and Immortality*', *Hibbert Journal*, LIX (July 1961). Also in *Christian Empiricism*, pp. 219–28.
6 'Some Further Reflections on *Freedom and Immortality*,' p. 354; *Christian Empiricism*, p. 226.
7 ibid., p. 354; *Christian Empiricism*, p. 226.
8 ibid., p. 355; *Christian Empiricism*, p. 227.
9 See his contribution to the symposium 'Paradox in Religion', *Proceedings of the Aristotelian Society*, Supplementary Vol. XXXIII (1959), pp. 219ff.; *Christian Empiricism*, pp. 98–119.
10 Ninian Smart, 'The Intellectual Crisis of British Christianity', *Theology*, LXVIII, no. 535 (January 1965), pp. 31ff.; *Christian Empiricism*, pp. 229ff. Anyone who reads both of Smart's articles here referred to will undoubtedly be struck by the inconsistency which he displays with regard to the relation of Ramsey's view to world religions. In the former article he complains that Ramsey's view is not broad enough to apply to other religions, while in the latter he maintains that Ramsey's view is compatible with too many other religions.
11 Paul van Buren, *The Secular Meaning of the Gospel*.
12 Ian Ramsey, 'Letter to the Editor', *Theology*, LXVIII, no. 536 (February 1965), pp. 109ff. Also in *Christian Empiricism*, pp. 237ff.
13 ibid., p. 110; *Christian Empiricism*, p. 238.
14 F. W. Dillistone (ed.). *Myth and Symbol*.
15 ibid., p. 87.
16 ibid., p. 89.
17 ibid., p. 90.
18 ibid., p. 91.
19 *Christian Discourse: Some Logical Explorations*, pp. 88–9.
20 ibid., pp. 87–91.

21 Paul van Buren *et al.*, 'Christian Education *Post Mortem Dei*', *Religious Education*, LX, no. 1 (January–February 1965), pp. 1–9. Also in *Christian Empiricism*, pp. 240ff.

22 Ramsey, 'Discernment, Commitment, and Cosmic Disclosures', *Religious Education*, LX, no. 1 (January–February 1965), pp. 10–14. Also in *Christian Empiricism*, pp. 250ff.

23 ibid., p. 12; *Christian Empiricism*, p. 253.

24 ibid., p. 13; *Christian Empiricism*, p. 255.

25 *Religious Studies* (June and September 1971).

26 ibid. (September), p. 225.

27 ibid. (September), p. 226.

28 *Religious Studies* (June 1973). See also her 'Some Aspects of Ian Ramsey's Empiricism', *International Journal for Philosophy of Religion* (Spring 1972).

29 ibid., p. 150.

30 ibid., p. 155.

31 *Journal of the American Academy of Religion* (September 1970), pp. 240ff.

32 ibid., p. 245.

33 ibid., p. 252.

34 ibid., p. 252.

35 Zenos Lectures.

36 *Christian Empiricism.*

Selected Bibliography

Note: The page references given in the notes of the text are to the American editions where both American and British publishers are cited.

IAN RAMSEY'S WORKS

'The Authority of the Church Today', *Authority and the Church*, ed. R. R. Williams (London, SPCK, 1965).

'Biology and Personality', *Philosophical Forum*, XXI (1964).

'The Challenge of Contemporary Philosophy to Christianity', *Modern Churchman*, XLII (1952).

'The Challenge of the Philosophy of Language', *London Quarterly and Holborn Review*, CLXXXVI (1961).

Christian Discourse: Some Logical Explorations (London, OUP, 1965).

Christian Empiricism (London, Sheldon Press, 1974).

(ed.) *Christian Ethics and Contemporary Philosophy* (London, SCM Press, 1966).

'Christianity and Language', *Philosophical Quarterly*, IV (1954).

'Contemporary Empiricism', *The Christian Scholar*, XLIII, no. 3 (Fall 1960).

'Discernment, Commitment, and Cosmic Disclosures', *Religious Education*, LX, no. 1 (January–February 1965).

'Empiricism and Religion: A Critique of Ryle's *Concept of Mind*', *The Christian Scholar*, XXXIX, no. 2 (June 1956).

'Ethics and Reason', *Church Quarterly Review*, CLVIII (April–June 1957).

'Facts and Disclosures', *Christian Empiricism* (London, Sheldon Press, 1974).

Freedom and Immortality (London, SCM Press, 1960).

'History and the Gospels: Some Philosophical Reflections', *Studia Evangelica: III* (Berlin), LXXXVIII (1964).

'Letter to the Editor', *Theology*, LXVIII, no. 536 (February 1965).

'The Logical Character of Resurrection-belief', *Theology*, LX, no. 443 (May 1957).

'A Logical Exploration of Some Christian Doctrines', *Chicago Theological Seminary Register*, LIII, no. 5 (May 1963).

'Miracles: An Exercise in Logical Mapwork', *The Miracles and the Resurrection* (London, SPCK, 1964).

Models and Mystery (London, OUP, 1964).

'Models and Mystery', Discussion: R. B. Braithwaite, J. Miller, T. Bastin; reply by Ramsey (*Theoria to Theory*, I, 1967).

Models for Divine Activity, Zenos Lectures, 1966 (London, SCM Press, 1973).

'On Being Articulate About the Gospel', *Chicago Theological Seminary Register*, LIII, no. 5 (May 1963).

On Being Sure in Religion (London, Athlone Press, 1963).

'On Understanding Mystery', *Chicago Theological Seminary Register*, LIII, no. 5 (May 1963).

Oral Communication, 13 July 1963, Seattle, Washington.

'Paradox in Religion', *Proceedings of the Aristotelian Society*, Supplementary Vol. XXXIII (1959).

'The Paradox of Omnipotence', *Mind*, LXV, no. 258 (April 1956).

Personality and Science, ed. Ian Ramsey and Ruth Porter (London, Churchill Livingstone, 1971).

'Persons and Funerals: What Do Person Words Mean?' *Hibbert Journal*, LIV (June 1956).

'Philosophy of Religion', unpublished lecture notes.

'Polanyi and J. L. Austin', *Intellect and Hope*, ed. T. Langford and W. H. Poteat (Duke University Press, 1968).

(ed.) *Prospect for Metaphysics* (New York, The Philosophical Library, 1961; London, George Allen & Unwin, 1961).

'Religion and Empiricism: III', *Cambridge Review*, LXXVII (1956).

'Religion and Science: A Philosopher's Approach', *Church Quarterly Review*, CLXII (January–March 1961).

Religion and Science: Conflict and Synthesis (London, SPCK, 1964).

Religious Language (New York, Macmillan, 1963; London, SCM, 1973).

'Some Further Reflections on *Freedom and Immortality*,' *Hibbert Journal*, LIX (July 1961).

'The Systematic Elusiveness of "I"', *Philosophical Quarterly*, V, no. 20 (July 1955).

'Talking About God: Models, Ancient and Modern', *Myth and Symbol*, ed. F. W. Dillistone (London, SPCK, 1966).

'Towards the Relevant in Theological Language', *Modern Churchman*, VIII (September 1964).

Words About God (New York, Harper and Row, 1971; London, SCM, 1971).

OTHER WORKS USED

Abernethy, G. L., and T. A. Langford (eds), *Philosophy of Religion* (New York, Macmillan, 1962; London, Collier-Macmillan, 1968).

Aquinas, St Thomas, *Summa Theologica*. Translated by Fathers of the English Dominican Province (Chicago, Encyclopedia Britannica, 1952; London, Eyre & Spottiswoode).

Austin, John L., *How To Do Things With Words* (Cambridge, Mass., Harvard University Press, 1962; London, OUP, 1971).

Austin, John L., *Philosophical Papers* (London, OUP, 1961).

Ayer, A. J., *Language, Truth and Logic* (New York, Dover Publications, 1943; Harmondsworth, Penguin, 1971).

Black, Max, *Models and Metaphors* (Ithaca, Cornell University Press, 1962).

Braithwaite, R. B., *An Empiricist View of the Nature of Religious Belief* (Cambridge, CUP, 1955).

Butler, Joseph, *The Analogy of Religion*, Vol. I of *Works* (Oxford, Clarendon Press, 1897).

Chappell, V. C. (ed.). *The Philosophy of Mind* (Englewood Cliffs and Hemel Hempstead, Prentice-Hall, 1962).

Cohen, Cynthia B., 'The Logic of Religious Language', *Religious Studies* (June 1973).

Egner, R. E. and Denonn, L. E. (eds), *The Basic Writings of Bertrand Russell* (New York, Simon and Schuster, 1961; London, George Allen & Unwin, 1961).

Evans, Donald, 'Ian Ramsey on Talk About God', *Religious Studies* (June and September 1971).

Ferré, Frederick, *Language, Logic and God* (New York, Harper and Row, 1961).

Ferré, Frederick, 'Mapping the Logic of Models in Science and Theology', *The Christian Scholar*, XLVI, no. 1 (Spring 1963).

Flew, Anthony, 'Can a Man Witness His Own Funeral?' *Hibbert Journal*, LIV (April 1956).

Flew, Anthony and Alasdair MacIntyre (ed.), *New Essays in Philosophical Theology* (London, SCM Press, 1955).

Foster, Michael, 'Contemporary British Philosophy and Christian Belief'. *The Christian Scholar*, XLIII, no. 3 (Fall 1960).

Foster, Michael, *Mystery and Philosophy* (London, SCM Press, 1957).

161

Gill, Jerry H., 'The Meaning of Religious Language', *Christianity Today*, IX, no. 8 (15 January 1965).

Gill, Jerry H., 'The Talk Circle', *The Christian Scholar*, XLIX, no. 1 (January 1966).

Gill, Jerry H., 'Wittgenstein and Religious Language', *Theology Today*, XXI, no. 1 (April 1964).

Hampshire, Stuart, *Thought and Action* (London, Chatto and Windus, 1959).

Hick, John (ed.), *Faith and the Philosophers* (New York, St Martin's Press, 1964).

Hick, John, *Philosophy of Religion* (Englewood Cliffs and Hemel Hempstead, Prentice-Hall, 1963).

Hick, John, 'Theology and Verification', *Theology Today*, XVIII, no. 1 (April 1960).

Hook, Sidney (ed.), *Religious Experience and Truth* (New York, New York University Press, 1961).

Hordern, William, *Speaking of God* (New York, Macmillan, 1964).

Hume, David, *A Treatise of Human Nature*, ed. L. A. Selby-Bigge (Oxford, Clarendon Press, 1949).

Hutchison, John, *Language and Faith* (Philadelphia, Westminster Press, 1963).

Kierkegaard, S., *Concluding Unscientific Postscript*, trans. David Swenson (Princeton, Princeton University Press, 1941).

Kierkegaard, S. *The Sickness Unto Death* (Garden City, Doubleday, 1955).

Kraft, Victor, *The Vienna Circle* (New York, Philosophical Library, 1953).

Lewis, H. D., 'Freedom and Immortality: A Review', *Hibbert Journal*, LIX (January 1961).

Mackie, J. L., 'Evil and Omnipotence', *Mind*, LXIV, no. 254 (April 1955).

McLain, F. M., 'From Odd-Talk to God-Talk?', *Journal of the American Academy of Religion* (September 1970).

Macquarrie, John, 'The Problem of Natural Theology', *Pittsburgh Theological Seminary Perspective*, V, no. 4 (December 1964).

Maurice, F. D., *Theological Essays* (New York, Redfield, 1854; Cambridge, J. Clarke, 1957).

Mitchell, Basil (ed.), *Faith and Logic* (Boston, Beacon Press, 1957).

Moore, G. E., *Philosophical Papers* (New York, Collier Books, 1962); London, George Allen & Unwin, 1959).

Pasch, Alan, *Experience and the Analytic* (Chicago, University of Chicago Press, 1958).

Polanyi, Michael, 'The Logic of Tacit Inference', unpublished paper.

Polanyi, Michael, *Personal Knowledge* (New York and London, Harper and Row, 1964. Originally published in 1958).

Polanyi, Michael, 'Tacit Knowing', *Reviews of Modern Physics*, XXXIV, no. 601 (1962).

Quine, W. V. O., *From a Logical Point of View* (New York and London, Harper and Row, 1963).

Quine, W. V. O., *Word and Object* (Massachusetts and London, MIT, 1960).

Randall, John H., *The Role of Knowledge in Western Religion* Boston, Beacon Press, 1958).

Randall, John H., 'Symposium: Are Religious Dogmas Cognitive and Meaningful?' *Journal of Philosophy*, LI, no. 5 (4 March 1954).

Ryle, Gilbert, *The Concept of Mind* (New York, Barnes and Noble, 1965; London, Hutchinson, 1967). Originally published in 1949.

Ryle, Gilbert, *Dilemmas* (Cambridge, CUP, 1954).

Sartre, Jean-Paul, *The Transcendence of the Ego* (New York, Noonday Press, 1957).

Smart, Ninian, 'The Intellectual Crisis of British Christianity', *Theology*, LXVIII, no. 535 (January 1965).

Smart, Ninian, 'Paradox in Religion', *Proceedings of The Aristotelian Society*, Supplementary Vol. XXXIII (1959).

Strawson, P. F., Chapter III in *Individuals: An Essay in Descriptive Metaphysics* (London, Methuen, University Paperbacks, 1959).

Strawson, P. F., *Introduction to Logical Theory* (New York, John Wiley, 1952; London, Methuen, 1967).

Tillich, Paul, *Dynamics of Faith* (New York, Harper and Brothers, 1958).

Tillich, Paul, *Systematic Theology* (Chicago, Chicago University Press, 1951; Welwyn Garden City, Nisbet, 1968).

Van Buren, Paul, *The Secular Meaning of the Gospel* (New York, Macmillan, 1964).

Van Buren, Paul *et al.*, 'Christian Education *Post Mortem Dei*', *Religious Education*, LX, no. 1 (January–February 1965).

White, Morton, *The Age of Analysis* (New York, New American Library, Mentor Books, 1955).

Wild, John, 'Is There a World of Ordinary Language?', *Philosophical Review*, LXVII, no. 4 (October 1958).

Wisdom, John, *Philosophy and Psycho-Analysis* (London, Blackwell, 1953).

Bibliography

Wittgenstein, Ludwig, *Philosophical Investigations*, trans. G. E. M. Anscombe (New York, Macmillan, 1953; Oxford, Blackwell, 1969).

Wittgenstein, Ludwig, *Tractatus Logico-Philosophicus*, trans. D. F. Pears and B. F. McGuiness (London, Routledge & Kegan Paul, 1961).

Zuurdeeg, Willem, *An Analytical Philosophy of Religion* (Nashville, Abingdon Press, 1961).

Zuurdeeg, Willem, 'Implications of Analytical Philosophy for Theology', *Journal of Bible and Religion*, XXIX, no. 3 (July 1961).

Index

Index